PARTS

By

Dominic Pimenta

First Printing, 2020

ISBN: 9798614558918
Imprint: Independently published

www.juniordoctorblog.com

Contents

"*While medicine is to be your vocation, or calling, see to it that you have also an avocation – some pastime which may serve to keep you in touch with the world of art, of science, or of letters.*"
William Osler

"*...the men and women merely players. They have their exits and their entrances; And one man in his time plays many parts*"
As You Like It (Act II, Scene VII).
William Shakespeare

For Dilsan, Ayla and Zach

Note: in order to preserve the absolute confidentiality of the patients in this book certain details, names and places have been changed or merged where necessary.

Introduction

Dear Reader,

Thank you for buying this book. As I sweep the proverbial dust from the manuscript and add this introduction, I've noticed there is a 'Part' missing from this book. The first, last and most human part of all; Time.

Time is a resource; we spend it, while it, pass it, waste it. As a doctor, I am reminded every day of how little some of us have, and how often that amount surprises us. As a father I have never been more aware of the passage of time; too quick, too little, moments you can never have again.

When I was a first-year medical student a group of us would all cook together every Sunday, mostly as (yet another) excuse to start drinking to be honest. As students this inevitably escalated. Firstly, every week had to have a theme, and the themes became ever-more tangential. One Sunday the clocks went back and the inevitable theme became time, or rather 'thyme'. Seriously. We made lasagne, added too much thyme to it and made it inedible. If only time could be so liberally added back to our lives.

Time is a most precious gift and we never see that more clearly than in our patients. Whether it's the few seconds that make a difference between life and death or the years a new cancer therapy might mean a patient can then spend with their family, medicine ultimately isn't about conquering disease. What we are really grappling with is time. To give a little more to our patients or to help make the most of what they have left. To find more for ourselves.

This book was born in a primordial soup of reflective rage as I left medicine but slowly evolved into a catharsis that showed me why I love it, and the way back. After pouring months of my life into these words, whole days of my time, I gave up and mothballed it. Only after several years do I realise the folly in that. We shouldn't be so flippant with our time as to wilfully waste it. I am also very conscious that there is a plethora of stories like these already out there. You may have had your fill of the voices of young doctors, but these stories aren't really ours; they belong to the patients we meet, the colleagues we count on, the infinite rolls of the dice that we call other human beings, no two are truly alike. So if you haven't had enough, here's "another bloody junior doctor book". And even if you have, 10% of your purchase today has been donated to the British Heart Foundation, funding life-changing research into heart disease, stroke and dementia.

All of which is to say I appreciate, perhaps more than some, how exceptionally precious your time truly is. So I am incredibly grateful you've decided to give a little to these particular pages. I hope you find it is well spent.

Dr Dominic Pimenta
February 2020

Alveoli

Breathe. Just breathe.
I'm 24 years old. I've been a qualified doctor for just twelve hours. A 28-year-old woman, Florence, minutes out of surgery, lies obtunded before me. Her breathing is too slow. The seconds between each breath seem to stretch lifetimes. In each pause, a crevasse opens that my whole career seems to fall into. Fourteen years of school, six years of university. I'm paralysed. I can't do this.
Breathe. I scream silently. Please just breathe.

**

Breathe. Just breathe.
I'm 30 years old. I've been a doctor for six years. A 44-year-old woman, April, admitted hours ago from the emergency department, lies before me. Her heart has stopped, suddenly and without warning. I'm standing in the eye of a maelstrom of activity. A dozen doctors and nurses swirl about me. An automated device pumps her heart brutally through her rib cage, a cardiac monitor beeps in tandem with each beat. This is my cardiac arrest team. We've been here for forty minutes. We've tried everything. As the leader, I break my silence only to give occasional directions. Internally my mind works furiously, going over everything over and over, correcting every potential problem, raking over every emergency algorithm. It's not enough.
I'm paralysed. We have nowhere to go but to wait. Nothing to do but to hope. Breathe. Just breathe.

**

The alveoli are tiny bubbles of lung tissue, so tiny a hundred and seventy of them will fit in a single cubic millimetre[1]. Normal human lungs have around 500 million[1] of these tiny alveoli and they are the site of exchange of gases in the body, the purpose of breathing. Their peculiar and wonderful anatomy means your healthy lungs have a total surface area between 30 to 70 square metres[2], the same as the total floor space of a small terraced house. With each breath, oxygen is extracted from the air and waste carbon dioxide from your bloodstream is excreted back out. The average person will take around 654 million[3] breaths in their lifetime.

At around 42 million breaths (aged 5) I decided I wanted to be a doctor. I can't honestly remember the specifics of that decision. After that, choosing medicine and going to medical school was a given. It has always felt a little like my life was on a rail, shuttling station to station; to school, college, med school, hospital.

For someone who decided early on to dedicate their lives to an emergency service I don't ever remember being particularly good in stressful situations. I can count the number of actual dire emergencies I'd been involved with up until day zero as a doctor on one hand.

1. My friend in college came off a trampoline and basically landed on me. I didn't so much as catch him as just not get out of the way. I don't think this counts as valour.

2. We ran out of petrol while driving through the mountains on the Arizona/California highway. I was about six. I believe my contribution was to wet myself.

3. We were arrested at the Brazilian/Argentine border for crossing illegally, albeit accidentally as well. I remember ratcheting through my Spanish dictionary looking up the word "lawyer" (abogado/a by the way) when fortunately, relatively speaking, a group of suspicious Brazilians behind us captured the authority's attention by trying to smuggle ten kilos of cocaine from Sao Paulo. With bigger fish on the hook they kicked us out with a fine.

So needless to say, I felt rather unprepared for the stakes to be so suddenly and permanently raised.

---

1 Ochs M, Nyengaard JR, Jung A, Knudsen L, Voigt M, Wahlers T, et al. The Number of Alveoli in the Human Lung. Am J Respir Crit Care Med. 2004 Jan 1;169(1):120–4.

2 Hasleton PS. The internal surface area of the adult human lung. J Anat. 1972 Sep;112(Pt 3):391–400.

3 At an average respiratory rate of 15 breaths per minute, over an average lifetime of 83 years.

My first ever day in a hospital as a fully-fledged doctor I was attached to a vascular surgery firm that dealt mostly with the consequences of diabetes on blood vessels in the limbs. I looked after patients who had lost, or were about to lose, a foot or a leg because of a loss of blood supply. We spent two days "shadowing" the doctors a year ahead of us, who were themselves just finishing their first year as medics. On the penultimate day in limbo between student and doctor the nurses had called me over to see Florence, a 28-year old lady who had come in for an abscess to be drained, a minor procedure but one that had required a general anaesthetic. The nurses were concerned as her oxygen levels were "a little low, doctor".

Now at medical school we practice emergency situations endlessly. We have acronyms and algorithms we chant, incantations to ward off catastrophe. DRABCDE[4]. Look, feel, listen, measure, treat, then repeat. Shockable, non-shockable. After a while they feel like mental gears, cogs that clink into place and we trot out rote learned responses like clockwork people. I remember a specific medical school exam with a dummy for a patient in a brightly lit clinical skills room, with this exact same situation. Through the rosy fallible spectacles of memory, the simulated patient was called Florence as well, although I know that must be a fabrication. In exam mode I fed the machine the scenario and cranked out the response.

"Check for danger. Is the patient responsive?"

"Look. Feel. Listen. Measure. Treat. Repeat."

It had felt so easy then.

Siobhan, an Irish sister in charge of the surgical unit, brought me back to earth.

"Come on now, let's see her?"

I remember craning to look down the length of the Surgical Assessment Unit, desperately hoping to see my swaggering, confident antecedent, the doctor I was following, Robert. Didn't Siobhan realise she'd collared the wrong guy? Like Peter Pan, I'm just the "shadow", I thought, not the real thing.

Florence was lying on the trolley, short mousy brown hair, pale and drowsy. The little probe on her finger snaked to a machine, bleeping a quiet alarm. Saturations: "89%." It was at this point I tried to access my internal clockwork. Behind my eyes the machine whirred, faltered and then cogs and springs pinged into the dark. Nothing. Limply I turned up the oxygen and just stood there. Paralysed. Breathe, I willed her silently to myself, please just breathe.

---

[4] Danger, Response, Airway, Breathing, Circulation, Disability, Everything else

It was at this point Siobhan appeared with an actual doctor, Robert, who I was supposed to be shadowing. Gently nudging me out the way he leapt into action, sitting her up, listening to her chest, speaking to her loudly but firmly to see how she responded. With a flick of his hand he looked into her eyes.

"Siobhan can I have some naloxone please?"

Siobhan, a senior surgical nurse of ten plus years, merely handed him the syringe she'd already prepared. A quick fiddle with the drip line and Florence gave a groan and sat forward.

Yawning she asked "Hello. Can I go home now?".

Robert reassured her and then made plans for her evening care.

"No more morphine, blood gas please and keep going on the oxygen, twenty minute observations, supportive care for now. We will review in a few hours."

Siobhan nodded and gave me a level look as she walked away.

Robert gave me a different, knowing, look.

"Pub?" He asked.

**

There is a whole science of dealing with emergencies, half psychology, half probability. The translation from the aviation industry to medicine isn't at all straightforward, but much of the lessons developed in cockpits can be applied to operating theatres and hospital wards. In his book, The Checklist Manifesto[5], US surgeon Atul Gawande described how the first modern era jet aircraft were at first a total disaster. They were simply too complex for a single pilot to fly without a catastrophic fatal error. Over time, the aviation industry developed a whole science based on a single premise; human beings unaided make frequent and avoidable mistakes. By using detailed checklists and rigorous drills, pilots managed to fly these complex machines without these avoidable errors, making travelling in a plane safer than driving a car. The checklist Dr Gawande and the World Health Organization pioneered for surgical procedures in the 2000s has likely saved hundreds of thousands of lives worldwide[6].

---

[5] Gawande A. The Checklist Manifesto: How to Get Things Right. Journal of Nursing Regulation. 2011 Jan 31;1:64.

[6] Up to a third reduction in surgical deaths in Scotland alone. Ramsay G, Haynes AB, Lipsitz SR, Solsky I, Leitch J, Gawande AA, et al. Reducing surgical mortality in Scotland by use of the WHO Surgical Safety Checklist. BJS (British Journal of Surgery). 2019 Jul 1;106(8):1005–11.

Medical school is full of guidelines and emergency algorithms to the same effect. Emergencies were always my biggest fear, about the only time as the most junior of doctors your mistakes can have a real impact. When the safety net is taken away and you're left holding the patient on the wire. What no one teaches you however is how to overcome your anxiety in that split second. How to breathe.

**

The day after was the day Florence was discharged, completely well, and also my first ever day as a full doctor. The full Peter Pan. The hospital was struggling, a small district general in the outer wards of a major city, serving one of the most deprived populations in the country. It was a difficult place to start.

I spent much of those first weeks alone, or at least what felt like being alone, including that first day. It was a blistering day in early August, and the ward was like a greenhouse. I did the ward round of my patients, six or seven elderly men and women who had recently had some part of their foot or toe removed. I examined them, looked at their drug charts and their blood results and then wrote my plan in their medical notes. Later that day I sat down with my registrar and talked about them. I went home that afternoon. No problems, no emergencies. Phew.

Over the next few months I thought a lot about that first day. I was terrified of emergencies. Terrified of not performing, of missing that vital something, of fumbling the catch and dropping the patient. I resolved to do something about it.

In hospitals we carry these antiquated devices called bleeps, pagers straight out of an early eighties Wall Street movie. Normally it's how we get called to some mundane task.

BLEEP. Dial the extension. "Can you rewrite a drug chart?".

BLEEP. Dial. "Can you speak to x-ray about Mr Carter's hip please?"

BLEEP. Dial. Engaged. Swear.

BLEEP. Ad nauseum.

Periodically, the bleep will make a different noise; a heart stopping ear-piercing blood curdling ringing and then a distorted voice;

"ADULT CARDIAC ARREST, WARD 9, ADULT CARDIAC ARREST, WARD 9."

That means somewhere in the hospital a patient's heart or lungs have stopped working. The alveoli hold about ten minutes of residual oxygen[7], but without a beating heart that oxygen cannot get to the brain. Every second without oxygen risks irreversible damage. That's why you might see doctors and nurses running in hospital corridors. I often hear patients talking about the doctor not getting to them quick enough. Trust me, you don't want to be the patient we are running towards.

I resolved the only way to overcome my fear was to run towards it. As a first year doctor I went to every cardiac arrest I could. The hospital I worked at was built on marsh land, meaning the entire place had to be laid out on a single floor along two tortuous corridors that crossed in the middle. From A&E at one end to maternity at the other it was nearly a kilometre. You quite quickly learnt the shortcuts.

One snowy day in mid-December the arrest call blared out at 7.30pm:
"CARDIAC ARREST, STROKE UNIT."
From the medical ward I was on it was a long way hurtling down three corridors to get there. Improvising I dashed out of the fire exit, planning to cut across the car park. I jumped a low wall, slipped on the ice and cracked my forearm on the way down. Nothing broken, but pretty cold and wet, I lurched on as fast as I could. Finding the fire exit closed on the other side, I pulled myself through an open window, bloody and dripping, sweating and panting, right onto the nurse's coffee table. A backwards "sorry" was all the shrieking nurses on break got by way of an explanation as I barged into the stroke ward next door, only to find the rest of the team already walking out, calmly chatting.

"False alarm" the anaesthetic registrar waved her hands at me, before seeing this haggard night terror gasping before her. Sympathetic to my idiocy, she led me to a chair.

"Breathe." She said, "Just breathe".

**

Whenever I think about those early days I always remember a story I was told by one of my surgical tutors.

---

[7] Strnad M, Lešnik D, Križmarić M. Arterial blood gas changes during cardiac arrest and cardiopulmonary resuscitation combined with passive oxygenation/ventilation: a METI HPS study. J Int Med Res. 2018 Nov;46(11):4605–16.

As a student he had struggled immensely with the sheer weight and complexity of anatomy. Far from merely learning the 206 bones of the adult human body, anatomy requires you to learn their relationships to each other, their nerves and blood vessels, their movements and muscles, their tendons and common diseases. The hand is made up of twenty-seven bones alone.

As a foreign student at a prestigious medical school he had felt the pressure to perform was immense. Failing an anatomy exam on the hand he began to lose faith in himself, and began to hate anatomy specifically with a passion. Undeterred he resolved to master his worst subject, to understand everything he could about his worst and most hated topic. Books, cadavers, models, whatever he could get his eyes on he studied and above all else, the hand. He found his fear, and he ran towards it. Twenty-five years later and the surgeon telling that story is an eminent orthopaedic surgeon. His specialty: complex hand trauma.

In retrospect I don't think I ever did very much at those early cardiac arrests. Those bleeps go out to the hardiest and most skilful junior doctors in the hospital: the anaesthetic registrar, the intensive care registrar, the medical registrar. I mostly just wrote down the events and kept time. Once I ran off with an urgent blood test. But just being there helped me overcome my fear. I started out hating cardiac arrests, and now I'm a cardiology registrar. Life is funny like that.

**

Flash forward six years and I'm standing at the head of a different bed, in a different hospital, a different lady.

Time stops and then skips forward, one minute like treacle, the next zipping by like oil. The middle-aged lady beneath the hands of the cardiac team is April. This is another arrest I've run to. I only know April from the notes, I only know her face as it is now, unresponsive, slack, eyes rolled up. Lifeless. Sometimes that's easier, but not this time.

Cardiac arrest cycles run in two minute intervals: cardiopulmonary resuscitation or CPR is commenced, the stopped heart is beat externally by hands placed in the middle of the chest, compressing the rib cage 100-120[8] times per minute. We do this in two minute cycles between which we reassess to see if their heart now beats for itself, if their lungs might breath for themselves. In those two minutes we look for a cause; why did this happen? Why is the heart not working? What could strike down a previously healthy middle-aged woman?

---

[8] Basic life support guidelines 2015. Resuscitation Council (UK).

I flick through the notes while another doctor recounts her story to me. April came in yesterday with vomiting. In the middle of winter stomach bug season was rampant and she'd been admitted for a simple drip overnight. This morning she had some pain in her chest and the next moment she collapsed to the floor.

Nothing about this makes much sense right now, but the clockwork gears are ticking away. From her electrical heart tracing it looks like she may have had a heart attack, or maybe a blood clot in the lungs. We've already run through the list of possible things to correct, and we are left with this one only. The treatment for either is the same: high doses of a very aggressive clot buster medication. However, this means we will have to wait an hour to see if it works. In the meantime, we place a machine on the chest to compress the heart for us, and we wait.

I sit and watch this young woman, nothing to do but wait, nothing left but to will her to breathe.

**

There are many causes of problems with the alveoli. They can fill up with fluid, blood, cancer or infection (pneumonia). They can become scarred and small and air struggles to pass through them or stretched and collapsed and air struggles to get down into the lungs to reach them. The blood supply can become blocked. If oxygen cannot get into the blood, it cannot get anywhere else. The brain, the heart, all of the organs will then swiftly fail. Breathing emergencies are some of the most severe and potentially deadly in medicine.

After ninety minutes of trying, way beyond what is normally attempted, April's heart starts to beat.

With a cry of suppressed triumph, I dash about trying to coordinate her care, to get her transferred and stabilised. A life saved. The team, some of whom are themselves on their "shadow" days, not quite yet doctors and visibly traumatised, are shaking with relief. I stop to think of the toll this has taken on everyone at the bedside.

Just as we are preparing her to move, her pulse plummets and flatlines again. There is no blood pressure. We try for a few more cycles, but there is no response. We have lost. We have failed. I have failed.

Time of death: 1.30pm. The world seems to rush back. "Who will speak to the family?" Someone asks.

All eyes turn to me.

**

It may come as no surprise to you that many health professionals, doctors and nurses, suffer from high rates of anxiety, depression and stress. Many quit entirely, leaving decades-long careers in the dust. This is "burnout". Coined in the '80s by US psychologist Prof. Christine Maslach "burnout"[9] has three defining elements; emotional exhaustion, cynicism with a decreased ability to care and a reduced belief in one's ability to do one's job at all. Reading that back, I can think of many times in my career to date I hit all three. Many walk away at this point. Some don't get to walk away at all. Each year we hear of high-profile cases as several (often junior) doctors[10] and nurses take their own lives.

How can we counter this? There's a move in recent years built on research from the military[11] to support medical professionals experiencing "stress injury" at work, to build effective "resilience". Figuring out how to support professionals in increasingly taxing conditions without losing staff is one of many great challenges facing the modern day NHS. However, there is only so much that can be asked of the staff. The sinister undertone to the emphasis on "resilience" is the pretence that the conditions in our hospitals and GP surgeries are inevitable, incontrovertible, like a natural disaster. This of course is not the case at all. Regardless, the translation of "resilience research" from the military is apt.

I remember those first days very much like being on the frontline of a battlefield. Not only the injuries, the human suffering, the relentless low-level anxiety coupled with intermittent spikes of pants-wetting stress, but also the camaraderie. The new doctors I started with, my fellow F1s, are still some of my closest friends today. I've been to their weddings and held their new-born children and they mine. There's a bond you form with your colleagues when you all go through the same trauma that keeps you going. It's important for us all to remember that the best "resilience" we can offer ourselves is other people, and to do the same for them.

**

A few hours later I sat down with April's family. I'm emotionally and physically exhausted.

---

[9] Maslach C, Schaufeli WB, Leiter MP. Job burnout. Annu Rev Psychol. 2001;52:397–422.

[10] Gerada C. Doctors and suicide. Br J Gen Pract. 2018 Apr 1;68(669):168.

[11] Brindley PG, Olusanya S, Wong A, Crowe L, Hawryluck L. Psychological 'burnout' in healthcare professionals: Updating our understanding, and not making it worse. J Intensive Care Soc. 2019 Nov;20(4):358–62.

I am often asked what the hardest part of the job is and the answer usually surprises. It's not the cardiac arrests or the sudden deaths or the day to day stressors of referrals or procedures. We have been trained for all those things from day one. The little clockwork machinery is all there for that. When the arrest bleep goes, the cogs start whirring. It's like you are on rails, no matter how dire the emergency.

It's this bit I find the hardest. I don't have any clockwork parts for a family's grief. Perhaps that's not a bad thing. I try to fall back on the methods I've been taught about explaining a condition; about how to break bad news. Like another checklist I try to tick the boxes; check their understanding, see what have they been told already, sign post, fire a warning shot, break the news, use silence, respond to their body language. All of this fails. Their teary eyes just stare blankly back at me. Two sisters, several nieces, a cousin, a pastor, a husband. I give up.

"Shall I just talk?"

They nod.

I try to explain slowly and simply what we think has happened, what we tried to do about it, and how we didn't succeed. I talk for what seems like an hour. I answer their questions as best I can, which mostly I cannot. I just let them know more information will come. I still don't know what happened to April.

When they have nothing left to ask or to hear again, I get up to leave.

"I'm so sorry again, we really did try everything we could" is what I try to say as I leave. But my voice cracks and I can't finish the sentence. For the first time in years I find myself tearing up at work. I excuse myself quickly.

Outside I tell myself to breathe. Just breathe.

Melanocytes

I grew up in a seaside village on the south coast of England, a town of fishing boats and bakeries, population approximately 10,000, mostly white, retirees.

My father, Leander, was born in 1940, four months into the Second World War, in Bombay as it was then. Being Indian Catholics the Pimentas originated in Bombay from the times when it was a Portuguese colony. He arrived in the U.K. via a childhood in Nairobi, Kenya. My mother, Deborah, was born in Chichester, twenty years my father's junior. Her mother, Patricia, my grandmother, was the daughter of a British Army soldier and British Raj mother whose family had been living in Colonial India since the 1860s. My grandmother was born in Bangalore in 1935. She fed us stories growing up of panthers prowling her bedroom window at night, kite hawks snatching chapatti from her open hand, servants and Gurkhas and mountains and leopards. Stories of British Raj India from both sides were a significant part of my childhood.

Needless to say, my four siblings and I growing up in a very English seaside town stood out. I remember smatterings of racist incidents: some older boys in the park, one or two run-ins at school. Once coming back through passport control as a child with my mum and despite us all sharing a surname the Border officer kept asking "Whose children are these?". I remember my mum being more upset than we were, being too young to really understand. It's a testament to the wonderful town I grew up in that my first real taste of racism came only when I entered the adult world.

As soon as I turned sixteen I got a job stacking the dairy aisle at my local Tesco. I can't say I enjoyed it very much. Working in retail is a lot like working in a hospital: you have to deal with people, even when they're not very nice, you have to work with other departments to deliver your job, even when they're not very nice, and winters are hellish.

The three days leading up to Christmas felt like Armageddon in the Home Counties. Whatever fad item (that year was goose fat, thanks Nigella) is fought over like the last water rations before a hurricane, queues at the checkouts back-up and block trolleys in the aisles, making the dairy aisle look like a cross between Supermarket Sweep and a spaghetti junction.

It's the day before Christmas Eve 2003, a little after lunchtime, and we are out of green top milk. What I can only describe as an angry mob is already forming without irony in the "chilled" section, waving garlic breads and Christmas crackers in place of pitchforks and torches. There's just two of us trying to fend off the fury of the middle-class horde; myself and a fellow part-timer a year older than me called Nat. I've just come back out from the warehouse, thanking God the lorry with the milk has arrived and is currently backing up for unloading. I try to appease the protestors; "just ten minutes now." Nat is being cornered by a silver haired red-faced man, his green gilet over his burgundy trousers creating the overall effect of a gigantic pheasant. He's gesticulating wildly as Nat cowers in front of him, trying to placate.

"I'm sorry sir the milk isn't available yet, the delivery is due later today." Nat is trying to say.

"Typical, just typical" he practically spits as he enunciates.

I try to jump in.

"Actually, the lorry is five minutes out, should be here shortly."

Mr Silver Pheasant turns on me.

"Oh?! Oh?! And she doesn't know anything because she's a woman eh? You Muslims are all the same!"

I can't recall the expression I made because we didn't have emojis back then, but I'm not sure whether I am offended or confused. I'm also sixteen years-old, have been working at Tesco for about two months, and have never been racially abused before by an adult.

Also this particular type of slur is a bit of a brain-teaser, like a double entendre of hate, and takes some processing to get to the insult. Mr Pheasant is gracefully defending the white girl's honour, the same white girl he up until that point had himself been abusing, from the brown, clearly Muslim (which I'm not but that's really not the point), wide-eyed sixteen-year-old medieval misogynist. What a guy.

I think my response was something like:

"No, seriously, the truck is in the yard."

And then I'm walking away, asking myself a question I'll ask over and over again for years to come. "Why is race such a problem?"

**

Being mixed race I have a rather non-specific appearance, meaning I've been assumed to be and/or abused for being from a whole spectrum of countries. Like a United Colours of Benetton advert if the rainbow began at dark chocolate and stopped at caramel. I've been wrongly profiled as Jamaican, Algerian, South African, Pakistani, Indonesian, Samoan, Italian, Israeli, Spanish, Portuguese, Mexican (a lot), Argentinian, Arab, Turkish, and once "from Hong Kong", which I can't really explain at all. I have a term for this international ambiguity: OmniBrown.

As a doctor I can't say that I've encountered much overt racism. Patients don't often commit to their discriminatory beliefs hard enough to refuse medical help. Maybe you got a better quality of racist in the old days, who knows? I've certainly had colleagues who have been though: a British GP I worked with of Nigerian descent was called to see a sick patient at home in the middle of the night, and when he duly arrived at 11pm the couple refused to let him in.

There is some subtle racism at work occasionally. When the consultant is confronted by a vaguely tanned patient and asks me do I speak Urdu or Portuguese or Farsi or Hindi ad nauseum. Occasionally when I speak to a colleague on the phone and then turn up in person and announce I'm the cardiology registrar there's a subtle double-take looking for a white male to match my voice. Sometimes there's even a not so subtle handshake with the nearest white male doctor before I can introduce myself. Sigh.

**

While your physical features are determined by a whole switchboard of genes that may or may not meet an imaginary category of a specific race, your skin tone is determined by a hundred and twenty or so genes that code for the activity of a certain cell type: melanocytes.

Melanocytes are spindly cells that sit in the uppermost layer of skin, the epidermis, and produce the skin pigments known as melanin. Each melanocyte[12] produces three types of skin pigment, a dark pigment, a lighter brown pigment and a reddish pigment, all three of which are present in different ratios. Melanocytes and their secreting bodies: melanosomes, are passed to other skin cells via tentacle arms called dendrites. The number of melanocytes in the human body varies at different sites in a single person, e.g. the palms and soles, but not between two people of different races. A man from Ghana (officially termed Fitzpatrick[13] scale VI: dark skin that doesn't burn) has the same number of melanocytes in their skin as a red-haired woman from Glasgow (Fitzpatrick scale I; pale skin that burns very easily). It is the amount and ratio of skin pigment and its distribution that determines skin tone, and ability to withstand high levels of UV radiation. Melanocytes make up only the tiniest fraction of all the cells in our body. Of an approximate total 40 trillion cells[14] there are around 2 billion melanocytes[15] in the skin of an average adult male, or 0.005% of the total. There is an absurd discordance between how big a part skin tone plays culturally and how literally small a part of ourselves it is biologically.

Beyond skin, human beings have very low levels of genetic diversity compared to most mammals, we share roughly 99.5%[16] of exactly the same DNA. There is more genetic variability between troops of chimpanzees[17] than the entire human race. From a biological perspective the differences between any of us are laughably tiny.

---

12 Lin JY, Fisher DE. Melanocyte biology and skin pigmentation. Nature. 2007 Feb 22;445(7130):843–50.

13 Fitzpatrick TB. The validity and practicality of sun-reactive skin types I through VI. Arch Dermatol. 1988 Jun;124(6):869–71. (On the same scale I'm about a Fitzpatrick IV in case you were wondering.)

14 Bianconi E, Piovesan A, Facchin F, Beraudi A, Casadei R, Frabetti F, et al. An estimation of the number of cells in the human body. Ann Hum Biol. 2013 Dec;40(6):463–71.

15 Szabo G. The regional anatomy of the human integument with special reference to the distribution of hair follicles, sweat glands and melanocytes. Philosophical Transactions of the Royal Society of London Series B, Biological Sciences. 1967 Sep 22;252(779):447–85.

16 1000 Genomes Project Consortium, Auton A, Brooks LD, Durbin RM, Garrison EP, Kang HM, et al. A global reference for human genetic variation. Nature. 2015 Oct 1;526(7571):68–74.

17 Bowden R, MacFie TS, Myers S, Hellenthal G, Nerrienet E, Bontrop RE, et al. Genomic Tools for Evolution and Conservation in the Chimpanzee: Pan troglodytes ellioti Is a Genetically Distinct Population. PLOS Genetics. 2012 Mar 1;8(3): e1002504.

As detailed in the book "How to Argue with A Racist"[18] by Adam Rutherford, the concept of race only appeared at all about four hundred years ago. While culturally race has huge connotations, on a scientific level the term is nearly meaningless. The genetics of a man from French Guiana have little in common with a man from Papua New Guinea, yet both are classed as "black." Similarly, "white" can be equally applied in different societal contexts to Argentinians, Armenians and Australians. 'Asian' is even more useless as a descriptor.

The use of race in medicine to risk stratify is a crude instrument, one we are already rapidly fine tuning. For example, using different medications in Afro-Caribbean people with high blood pressure is based on valid scientific data, but that's a generalisation and once we drill down to the genomics of that effect we will dispense with it, as we already do with a whole host of other gene-specific drug reactions.

Growing up brown in a very white town gave me an outsider's perspective of race. Being "mixed" I can't readily identify as Asian or White, I am something in between, which strikes me as too simplistic a description of who I am and therefore invalid.

I suppose I never really had a "tribe" in the traditional sense, so I struggle to understand tribal behaviour that trumps logic or compassion. I've never really felt anything other than British, but even then at the fringes of the tribe. Medicine is itself its own tribe; it holds arcane knowledge, admittance is exclusive and it possesses a specific value set; humanitarianism, justice, autonomy and benevolence. A code which is mandatorily enforced in law and regulation. When I became a medic for the first time I felt I had a tribe of my own.

And what a diverse tribe it is. One in ten NHS staff were born abroad. Much of my knowledge about other cultures in the world comes from working alongside colleagues born abroad: Italy, Ghana, Eritrea, Peru, Denmark, India, Singapore, Portugal, Russia, Latvia, South Africa, Canada, USA, Philippines, China, Cyprus, Ireland.

As a very junior doctor working night shifts I always found great refuge in our cardiac care unit which was coincidentally nearly entirely staffed by Filipino nurses. They were amongst the warmest, most competent and professional nursing colleagues I've ever had. They always knew what to do in the worst situations, especially when I didn't. A few years later we ended up briefly staying in a Filipino neighbourhood in London, and I was surprised by how naturally I felt at home there, having worked so closely with so many people from the Philippines in the NHS.

---

[18] Rutherford A. How to Argue with a Racist: What Our Genes Do (and Don't) Say About Human Difference. S.l.: The Experiment; 2020. 224 p.

Our views on race are profoundly shaped by our human relationships. We are very fortunate in the health service to share some of the deepest human moments with our patients, and doubly fortunate we work so closely in a diverse environment that can teach us how universal that humanity truly is.

**

In our current fevered climate, we swim in a deluge of misinformation about immigrants and 'health tourists'. As I drove to work one winter's day as a junior cardiology registrar, the topic of that morning's radio phone-in was exactly that, proposing all patients would need to present their passport or a credit card before getting treatment. Quite aware of both the inordinate amount of administration we already have to do, and appalled at the dehumanising tone of the callers, I pulled over and decided to call in. In the back of my mind I was thinking about Zara.

Zara had been the first patient on my ward round a few weeks' prior, a sixty-year-old lady from Lahore in Pakistan, visiting family in the UK. Zara had an extensive history of heart disease, which her brother kindly translated: she'd had stents placed in her coronary arteries and valves replaced which had slightly weakened her heart. After the first stent failed she went on to have open heart surgery to fix it. Her list of medications was long and all in brand names I didn't recognise. I had to spend ten minutes Googling them. Zara had been working hard in a roasting kitchen helping prepare a family meal when she felt a central pain in her chest. Her brother tells me it felt "crushed", and ran down her left arm and into her jaw, for thirty minutes. Zara's electrical heart tracing and blood tests confirmed my suspicions: she'd had another major heart attack.
The only problem was Zara wasn't a UK citizen and might normally have to pay for any routine UK treatment. She had travel insurance but the family were desperate to know if they would be billed: her brother drove a taxi and lived in a rough estate on the edge of the borough, they didn't have a spare £10,000 to pay for cardiac care. As an emergency case, Zara was entitled, but I didn't know the specifics. I told them I would try and find out.
Later that day I heard the department that deals with non-NHS patients, known as the overseas team, had come to see Zara while her brother had returned home, and after a brief conversation Zara self-discharged against medical advice.

I was livid. A doctor should've been present. I don't know what was told to Zara or how that conversation was handled; did she have a translator? Did she understand the risk to her life of discharging after a heart attack? What did the Overseas team (generally a nurse or lay person) tell her about her condition? An acute heart attack is a potentially life-threatening event, and would normally be covered, but it was too late. I'd like to tell you this was a one-off event, but I've seen it many times over; patients entitled to treatment scared into declining or leaving by finance officers. I have no issue with a patient from overseas being charged appropriately for elective medicine, but not at the cost of some patients being declined overzealously, to their harm.

I don't know what happened to Zara. She could've had another major heart attack at her brother's house and been taken to another hospital (at exponentially greater cost to the NHS), she could've had a heart event at the airport or on the plane at a greater cost still. I hope she made it back to Lahore safe and sound and to her regular doctor, but it still gnaws at me that I don't know and I can't say for sure she didn't die over a poorly translated conversation about money.

**

I tried to get some of these points across to the host; that we waste more time and money trying to recover money from the very rare 'health tourists' we see in the NHS (<0.3% of the budget) than we ever actually recover from them. While in the crossfire we harm patients like Zara and many others, vulnerable due to language barriers, worried about bankrupting their families. I fear these points fell on deaf ears, but perhaps someone was listening out there.

**

There's a unique perspective to be gained by physically looking beyond the surface of a human being. It's hard to believe that skin colour is such a differentiator when you've seen how everyone's spleen is an identical shade of rich scarlet, how all of our blood is the same deep merlot, how all of our brains are the same shade of creamy pink. I wish the world could share that perspective. I know it sadly does not.
People occasionally ask me what race or ethnicity I'll tell my children they are. Technically they are one quarter Indian-Portuguese, one quarter English-Irish, one quarter Turkish-Cypriot and one quarter Turkish-Mainland. I don't want to teach my kids they have to be pigeon-holed into regressive stereotypes. I always reply proudly in the same way.

"I'll tell them they're Londoners."

Mortis

The beginning of life as a doctor starts with the end.

It's 2006, I'm 19 years old and I'm standing nervously bouncing foot-to-foot with a gaggle of fellow white coats. I've never worn the white coat before, it's brand new, so crisp it chafes slightly on my bare arms. It was bought for a specific purpose, to be worn only at a specific time in a specific place. The doors open with a gust of sickly formaldehyde. We fall silent and file inside. This is the one class we are all dreading. This is human dissection.

The room is lined with anatomical specimens, from floor to ceiling sit all manner and shape of fluid filled jars. Colossal tanks filled with pairs of lungs and massive tumour-filled livers to bleak tiny beakers, no bigger than a jam jar, containing staring eyeballs and foetuses in the earliest stages of development. The collection is hundreds of years old. On twenty trolleys dotted throughout the room, twenty human shapes lie beneath white drapes.

The anatomy demonstrator gives a brief introduction and then the drapes are pulled away. Someone always faints, we've been told. I'm standing two feet away from our body, a man in his late seventies, head still covered but otherwise bare, his skin is yellowed, waxen, bloated. You could almost believe this wasn't real, in a world where nearly nothing is. For reasons I still can't quite fathom I take the man's hand, hold it like I would a friend. It feels cold, like a mannequin but denser, heavier. Like a visual illusion, suddenly I see him change. From "cadaver" to person. Here lies a father or a grandfather, a husband or a brother. A whole lifetime of experiences and relationships. At least here is their body, so recently vacated. Where are they?

A yelp and loud gasps of excitement break my reverie; someone has fainted. I let go of his hand and death rushes back. Someone always faints.

**

Many years later I stand nervously in the corner of a hospital lift. I've been a doctor for six years. I've worked in intensive care and oncology; I've seen more than my fair share of patients die. It seems to be the one part of the job I can't get used to. Especially in circumstances like this.

It's the middle of a Monday morning, and the lift is empty. This hospital is a stack of wards fifteen stories high. Today I'm heading to the morgue. Standing alone as the lift carries me to the basement feels as if I'm traversing the veil, descending into the underworld.

Trevor had been a bright 70-year old ex-brickie, full head of thick grey hair, missing one or two teeth, deeply tanned from years in the sun. A huge tattoo of the Tottenham Hotspurs cockerel and ball had adorned his right shoulder. My local team, I'd made sure his bedside TV had been working to watch the highlights that weekend.

Trevor came in with chest pain three days earlier. A lifelong smoker, "halfway to a hundred and forty" as he put it, he actually had stayed remarkably healthy. He had been wiry and tough and unrelentingly cheerful. When I told him his blood markers and electrical tracings looked like he'd had a large heart attack he'd shrugged. "Overdue isn't it doc?". I tried to get him to stop smoking, he'd said he would try. Minutes later he nipped out for a cigarette. Outside he told me "the stress of quitting was getting to me", with a wry smile. I told him he needed to stay put on the ward, but he wasn't a man to do anything other than what he wanted. I liked Trevor a lot.

While waiting for his angiogram, a test and treatment for blocked heart arteries, Trevor nipped out again after the match, a summery Sunday evening. When he came back, he told the nurse he had a twinge of pain in his chest. Then he collapsed to the floor. Despite the best efforts of the team, he didn't get up again.

Now I was heading to the morgue to certify Trevor's death. The last time I'd seen him he'd been happily smiling, ebullient about Spurs' chances this year. This image is still in my head when the mortuary assistant rolls out his body from the refrigerated unit.

Thankfully his eyes are closed. I examine the body as per my legal requirement. The recently deceased don't feel like those prepared for dissection. Their tissue feels human. I still can't get used to this.

"Sorry Trevor" I think quietly to myself.

**

Most of the population in the developed world will die in a hospital or a hospice. The reality of modern medicine is although we can do more and more, we can't keep people alive forever. Nor should we try. We often think of a patient dying as a failure. In fact, the opposite is true. In an oft-quoted study of patients that've died in hospital ~97% of patient deaths were deemed likely "unavoidable"[19]. That's not to say we don't take a patient's death lightly. Far from it. An unexpected death triggers an extensive investigation. But it does suggest that perhaps we should be more comfortable talking about death, and what to do when one of us, or someone we love, is in the last throes of an illness. Many want "everything done" right up until the last, and even beyond. Trying to "bring them back", or resuscitate. One of the hardest parts of any doctor's job is talking to patients about the end of life, and whether to try to resuscitate them or not. I often wish I could have these conversations far away in space and time from the moment a patient is actually ill. So let's talk about it now.

When I sit down with a patient or their family to discuss resuscitation I always find their understanding of CPR very different from mine. We always start with the same questions. What is CPR? It stands for cardiopulmonary resuscitation, which simply means, trying to restart (resuscitation) your heart (cardio) or lungs (pulmonary). In other words, if you get so sick that your heart or your lungs stopped working, we would try to restart them.

How do we do that? Well, the process of CPR is actually quite brutal. To pump a heart that isn't beating you have to compress it from the outside, 100-120 times a minute. To do it properly you need to squeeze the chest by 1/3 of its depth, or 5-6 cm deep[20]. This sometimes breaks ribs. Trust me, it's as horrific as it sounds.

The next step is stripping the clothes, and placing two large electrodes onto the chest connected to a monitor and large battery that can give an electric shock. If there is a heart rhythm that can be shocked, we dial up the machine to a high energy setting, tell everyone to not touch the patient or they will get shocked themselves, and electrocute them. I've seen this in semi-conscious patients and it hurts. We then carry on with pounding on the chest. At some point a specially trained doctor or nurse will try and pass a breathing tube into your throat, insert tubes into the veins in your arms, neck or groin, and give large doses of heart pumping drugs.

[19] Hogan H, Healey F, Neale G, Thomson R, Vincent C, Black N. Preventable deaths due to problems in care in English acute hospitals: a retrospective case record review study. BMJ Qual Saf. 2012 Sep;21(9):737–45.

[20] Basic life support guidelines 2015. Resuscitation Council (UK).

We cycle through this process, deciding every two minutes whether the heart can be shocked, or whether there is something else we can do. This can go on for some time. We swap the person giving compressions back and forth so they don't get tired. Like with April, we even have a machine that does this for us.

At some point we will have tried everything. Resuscitation stops when every single member of the team agrees there is nothing more to do, or the patient's heart starts beating again on its own.

What happens next? If the patient's heart or lungs started working again, then the breathing tube is connected to a machine, and the patient is taken to intensive care.

I've looked after lots of patients who went through this. Some will leave the hospital, many won't.

The reason being is that for every second your brain is without oxygen your brain cells are dying. We can see this on an MRI scan after a long period of 'downtime'- time without oxygen or blood pumping leaves your brain swollen and misshapen. The chance of recovery is slimmer the worse the damage appears to be.

That all sounds very doom and gloom, but it shouldn't. This is the very last ditch attempt to save life, and its value is inherent in the few successes we have. But they are few.

I wish everybody knew how few. The problem is our understanding of CPR as a society is based entirely on commercials and television. A study[21] many years ago found that on television nearly half of resuscitation scenarios end with the patient waking up and hurrahs all round. But this is far from reality.

If you are already in hospital, the chance of the average person waking up and leaving hospital unharmed after a 'cardiac arrest' is only 18%[22], or 1 in 5. If you have a cardiac arrest at home, it's as low as 2%[23], or 1 in 50. That is probably news to you. It certainly was to me at medical school. It's news to most of my patients and their families.

In summary, CPR is a brutal last ditch process that only sometimes works and usually has significant and lasting harms for the few that do survive. You may think I'm being grim but this is the honest truth, please ask any medical professional.

---

21 Harris D, Willoughby H. Resuscitation on television: realistic or ridiculous? A quantitative observational analysis of the portrayal of cardiopulmonary resuscitation in television medical drama. Resuscitation. 2009 Nov;80(11):1275-9.

22 Ofoma UR, Basnet S, Berger A, Kirchner HL, Girotra S, Investigators for the AHAGW the G-R, et al. Trends in Survival After In-Hospital Cardiac Arrest During Nights and Weekends. J Am Coll Cardiol. 2018 Jan 22;71(4):402-11.

23 Perkins GD, Ji C, Deakin CD, Quinn T, Nolan JP, Scomparin C, et al. A Randomized Trial of Epinephrine in Out-of-Hospital Cardiac Arrest. New England Journal of Medicine. 2018 Aug 23;379(8):711-21.

Now, that's why I always want to talk about CPR when people are well. When things are very hectic and somebody is very sick, it's hard to listen to someone saying the chance of success of CPR is low. It sounds like we are giving up. But we are not, we are making a plan. Good doctors like plans. We call this plan a 'do not attempt CPR' order, or DNACPR. It's a very important bit of paper, kept at the front of the patient's notes or as an alert screen on the electronic record, usually an obvious colour like red. It states very clearly that if the heart or lungs stop working we should not try to restart them, and the reasons why.

It doesn't change any decision about having an operation, or chemotherapy, or even using life support machines. It's not about changing the course of treatment; it's about making a plan for if it all goes wrong.

It might surprise you to know that a higher proportion of doctors who become unwell utilise palliative care more than the general population[24], perhaps understanding the limits of modern medicine better. Many doctors have their red line conditions, things they have seen that they themselves would never want to go through the treatment for, knowing the suffering involved and the likely outcomes.

There's a great book about medicine and death called "Being Mortal" by an American surgeon called Atul Gawande[25]. In it he talks about five questions that everybody should ask when they contemplate the end of their lives, and he sums them up with one question "what are you fighting for?"

Reading this at home, hopefully very well, it might be hard to ever imagine what you would want if you became very sick. What would you fight for? Please think about it.

We aren't very good as a society about talking about death, as if the discussion of the inevitable somehow diminishes the possible. I wish I was better at it. Perhaps one day I'll get used to it. Perhaps not.

---

[24] Wunsch H, Scales D, Gershengorn HB, Hua M, Hill AD, Fu L, et al. End-of-Life Care Received by Physicians Compared With Nonphysicians. JAMA Network Open. 2019 Jul 24;2(7):e197650–e197650.

[25] Gawande A. Being Mortal: Illness, Medicine and What Matters in the End. Profile Books Ltd; 2015. 296 p.

Olfaction

As a doctor and a relatively new father for the second time, I seem to spend far too much time thinking about poo. At work we stare into poo, sample poo, compare poo to a line-up of seven types of poo and decide exactly which type of excrement has been produced. At home you become unhealthily obsessed with your baby's dirty nappies; "is it enough, is it too much, what is that?!" I'm sure the combination of parent and doctor only makes this so much worse.

In such a sanitised culture dealing with bodily fluids is a rite of passage, one that breaches the skein between the layman and the arcane. It's easy to let that seep into one's home life; talking about poo over the dinner table is, unfortunately, a frequent bad habit.

Looking after humans is a messy business, which can often offend the senses. The human process of "smelling" or olfaction is fascinating. Olfaction is the detection of molecules in the air called odorants.[26] These float into your nose and dissolve into the mucous there, where they are bound by cells connected directly to your brain via a nerve called the olfactory nerve.

I'm rather blessed in a way by having a poor sense of smell. It's an unforeseen gift in the hospital and occasionally at home as well. I'm not sure how my more able-nosed colleagues cope sometimes, although I have to admit, smell can sometimes be useful to make a diagnosis. I had a senior when I was starting out who seemed to be part Basset hound. We'd walk onto the ward, he'd cock his head back dramatically and sniff the air. "Someone has had a stomach bleed" he would say, and rush around to the source of the smell to confirm his olfactory suspicions. We'd find a bedpan full of black and offensive diarrhoea, a clear sign of internal blood that had been partially digested in the gut. He was right every time.

---

26 Menini A, Lagostena L, Boccaccio A. Olfaction: From Odorant Molecules to the Olfactory Cortex. Physiology. 2004 Jun 1;19(3):101–4.

In fact, the human nose was an essential tool to the early modern physicians. The "fruity" odour of diabetic ketoacidosis, a life-threatening lack of insulin, or the sickly sweet smell of gas gangrene, a severe infection of dying tissue, were textbook odours every doctor had to know[27]. In the modern era experiments with animals and even synthetic "noses" have diagnosed everything from Parkinson's disease[28] to tuberculosis[29] to cancer[30] by "smell" alone. However, given the alternative less useful and far worse smells I have to deal with on a daily basis, I'm happy with my nasal ability as it is.

As a student doctor I soon cottoned on to how useful this minor deficit was. Attached to a general surgical team, I once stood in an operating theatre with the anaesthetised patient ready for bowel surgery on the table, senior surgical registrar seated at the literal bottom end, getting the patient placed in the lithotomy position, legs wide. All was routine so far, except the patient hadn't been given the proper colon clearing medication beforehand, and when the nurses lifted the patient's legs, like pressing on the lever of a Mr. Whippy ice cream dispenser, the rise in abdominal pressure pushed about half a foot of poo out and onto the surgical registrar, softly curling on his lap while the operating theatre looked on in stunned silence. Entirely coincidentally, that was the day I decided against becoming a surgeon.

It's not just faeces; healthcare professionals see and smell far too much of other people's bodily fluids. Vomit is a particularly popular one: we like to peer into it for bile or blood or granules. I looked after a young man that had vomited 10-15 times a day for two years. It was impossible to go near his bedside without at least one or two bowels of vomit to inspect. He was eventually diagnosed with cyclical vomiting syndrome due to chronic marijuana abuse.

We deal with blood a lot, for obvious reasons. They say if you can't stand the sight of blood you shouldn't involve yourself in healthcare, but I had a roommate at university who used to faint at a paper-cut, ten years later he is an anaesthetist, sitting watching the goriest and bloodiest operations you can imagine, every single day. Quite quickly the alien and revolting becomes the mundane and routine.

[27] Bijland LR, Bomers MK, Smulders YM. Smelling the diagnosis: a review on the use of scent in diagnosing disease. Neth J Med. 2013 Aug;71(6):300-7.

[28] Mahlknecht P, Pechlaner R, Boesveldt S, Volc D, Pinter B, Reiter E, et al. Optimizing odor identification testing as quick and accurate diagnostic tool for Parkinson's disease. Mov Disord. 2016;31(9):1408-13.

[29] Cambau E, Poljak M. Sniffing animals as a diagnostic tool in infectious diseases. Clin Microbiol Infect. 2019 Nov 14;

[30] Janfaza S, Banan Nojavani M, Khorsand B, Nikkhah M, Zahiri J. Cancer Odor Database (COD): a critical databank for cancer diagnosis research. Database (Oxford) [Internet]. 2017 Aug 3 [cited 2020 Feb 12];2017. Available from: https://www.ncbi.nlm.nih.gov/pmc/articles/PMC5737198/

It can become unhealthy. One of my previous bosses, a consultant professor who is one of the foremost leaders in his field internationally, had a most peculiar favourite past time when the ward was quiet. He'd like to swap stories about his halcyon days in emergency departments, in a game called "Who Found What Up Someone's Bottom". As wild and weird as it may seem, what people put inside their bottoms and then have to seek medical attention about is grotesquely fascinating. He had some amazing stories.

A light bulb, a Victorian antique clock, still ticking, a whole candlestick, plus candle. He would win this game often. He had to concede defeat however when one of the doctors, fresh from a stint abroad, trumped us all. An entire coconut, whole and unbroken. It might seem crass to laugh about these things, but how else do you process the stream of the bizarre and tragic humanity you are exposed to if not laugh about it?

Generally, I personally never had a problem with the messier side of medicine. I was okay with vomit and faeces, sputum and urine, but I sometimes wobbled with blood.

**

It's 2010 and I'm a student on an obstetrics rotation at a large and run-down district general hospital. As students we spend three years moving specialties every six weeks to gain a basic but rounded experience of all aspects of medicine. Today I am helping to deliver a baby. I'm standing in an operating theatre, sterile in blue scrubs, masked and ready to assist. The tension is palpable.

Fatma is lying on the table before us. She's thirty-six weeks pregnant with her second child, her first a bright and cheeky five-year-old boy I'd seen running around the corridors with his dad. She had lost another baby in between and this was her third and planned to be last pregnancy.

At around twenty weeks Fatma had gone in for her routine scan, and came out in floods of tears. There was a problem with the baby. Or more accurately, there was a problem with the single most vital organ a baby shares during its time in the womb: the placenta.

The placenta is the interface between mother and child through which flows all of the nutrients, oxygen, white blood cells, red blood cells and everything else that feeds the growing foetus. A bag of blood vessels, at term about the size of a deep pan pizza, the placenta receives three-quarters of a litre of blood every minute[31], back and forth between maternal and baby circulation. Usually the placenta sits at the apex of the uterus, and comes away when the baby is delivered. The uterus contracts down and the mother's body clamps off the vascular supply so she doesn't immediately bleed out. Without these mechanisms the mother could lose her entire circulation of blood in minutes.

Fatma's placenta was in the wrong place. It lay over the opening of the uterus, meaning the baby couldn't get out. Worse still, part of it lay around the very top of the uterus closest to the skin, meaning the only way to get the baby out was by caesarean, and the only way to perform a caesarean in Fatma was to cut **through** the placenta.

That's exactly what we are about to do. Ms Warren, the consultant, is in one corner of the theatre, a porter ready with a coolbox full of bags of blood in the other. The junior doctor about to do the procedure is nearly a consultant herself. Christie is returning from twelve months' maternity leave and this is one of the first operations she's performed since returning. I'm as junior as it can get and I know this is high risk surgery. Christie doesn't show it though. Her long fingers move with efficient purpose as she prepares the skin. It's my hands that are shaking, holding the retractors as she makes the initial incision. The theatre is both far more crowded and far quieter than I'm used to. You could hear a pin drop as Christie pauses, scalpel hovering just above the uterus. She takes the slightest breath in, and then makes a smooth incision across its length. The blood pours out in a way I've never seen, a crimson wave surges out of Fatma's open abdomen, over the table and onto the floor. I feel it's warmth as it washes over my surgical wellington boots. They told me to wear boots. It looks exactly like the lift opening in that infamous scene from The Shining. A literal river of blood.

31 Wang Y, Zhao S. Placental Blood Circulation [Internet]. Morgan & Claypool Life Sciences; 2010 [cited 2020 Feb 12]. Available from: https://www.ncbi.nlm.nih.gov/books/NBK53254/

I feel faint, and for a moment I am not sure if I'm holding the retractors or hanging on to them to keep me up. The blood doesn't stop. Ms Warren is moving coolly in the periphery, but my vision is narrowing. All I can see now is Christie's hands, moving faster than I can track as the blood keeps coming. My arms feel heavy and my head feels light as Christie reaches in and wrenches out a small purple podgy bundle, covered in blood. The midwife whips the new-born away and out of sight. I hear a loud angry cry. I feel the tension ease in the room a little. Crying babies are a very good thing. It's quiet new-borns we worry about.

Christie ignores everything, still working furiously. I can see she's flustered and I wonder if this is going well. There's so much blood I can't really tell. I concentrate on not passing out, holding the retractors wide as I can manage, my arms numb, my stomach back flipping. Am I going to vomit?

This feels like the end of my career, a five-line footnote in the Daily Mail: London medical student vomits into open abdomen, immediately expelled and jailed.

A scrub nurse pokes me in the back.

"Hey, you okay?" She's looking concerned. Ms Warren catches my eye and I notice she's now scrubbed into a surgical gown herself. She looks like she's about to step in, but there's no need.

Christie, oblivious to all this and rightly so, breathes a sigh of relief. Without looking up she says.

"You can relax those retractors now"

I let go and hand them back to the scrub nurse. The blood has stopped, Christie is closing up, the new little girl is quietly looking up at her mum for the first time, Fatma's numbers look okay and I look down and see what must be litres of blood on the floor. That woozy feeling knocks me back again and I have to sit down. I de-scrub and leave. Outside I bump into Christie, clearly exuberant about how well it all went.

"Thanks for your help." She says, grinning into her coffee. Up close her mousy brown hair is plastered to her forehead, her cheeks are still flushed, her handshakes now imperceptibly. She's clearly exhausted after the adrenaline.

"That was. Crazy." I stammer. "How did you keep it together?"

She shrugs. "You get used to it."

**

I never really had a problem with blood after that, but to be honest I've never seen anything like it since. Christie was right, you do "get used to it". You get used to dealing with all the messiest parts of other people; their blood, their vomit and all the other s**t, literally and figuratively.

Craig was 36, a zealous bodybuilder, a husband and a father, a regular steroid user and occasional cocaine sampler, a part-time DJ, full-time carpenter and a self-professed Nazi. His swastika tattoo, one of a dozen, rather gave it away. I first met Craig on the cardiology ward, where he told me he "didn't mind us talking" but he'd rather I'd see if a white doctor would look after him instead. He'd abused the nurses overnight, telling the Filipino nurses to "f**k off back home" and the black nurses to "take their dirty hands off him."

This wonderful man had been admitted overnight, gasping for breath, his whole body bloated and swollen. I flicked through his X-rays; his lungs were swimming in fluid and his heart was pathologically dilated. Despite his protestations Craig was in a bad way that morning, he needed extra oxygen to breathe at all and the tissues in his legs and thighs were choked with fluid, even his scrotum was painfully ballooning with water, stretched to the size of a grapefruit. Having dealt with various Craigs in the past, I started out by ignoring all of his abuse and vitriol and cutting straight to the medicine.

"How long have your legs been like this?" I asked, as I pushed a thumb onto his shin. It left an impression two centimetres deep, like pressing into dough. This was the same right up to his nipples. Craig was drowning inside his own body.

He looked nervous.

"A couple of months."

"How many pillows do you have to sleep with now?" I asked. An odd question, and one I know will disconcert him. He has all the signs of severe heart failure. These patients struggle to breath lying flat, as the excess fluid settles in their lungs when they are on their back.

Craig's beady brown eyes narrow in his square face.

"I'm up to four now."

I can see I'm making headway, establishing something of a rapport by making him think I'm Sherlock Holmes.

"How often do you wake up at night gasping for air?" Another odd question, a bit more of a long-shot. A typical symptom of heart failure but not as common. It hits home. Craig's eyebrows shoot up.

"Uh...most nights"

I nod sagely as I move to examine him. He's a massive guy, six foot two and about the same as wide. The pulsation in his neck shoots to his ears with each beat of his heart. It's so visible I take students back later and ask them to tell me his heart rate from the end of the bed alone. I listen to his lungs, they crackle with fluid at the top, and the breath sounds disappear at the bottom. Fluid is accumulating around the outside of the lungs as well.

I know I have Craig's attention now, despite not being a "white doctor" when he asks; "Does it look bad, doc?"

I know he's worried, and in his concern for his health he has forgotten his prejudices.

"It's too early to say what the cause is, but it does look like your heart isn't beating very well. Do you mind if I do a quick scan?"

Nazi Craig has vanished, his racist bravado dissipating like so much smoke. Frightened, human Craig nods meekly. I grab the bedside echo machine and as soon as I place it on Craig's chest I can see what I already know: Craig's heart is barely beating at all.

**

I broke the news to Craig like I would any other patient. Slowly, compassionately, checking he understood, explaining the plan; an MRI scan of his heart, water medication to get rid of the fluid, a cocktail of medications to stabilise his heart. I asked gently about his drug habits, explaining they may have caused this. He admitted to snorting cocaine, taking anabolic steroids and drinking too much alcohol. I believed him when he said he didn't inject any drugs. I gave him some more information about the plan, checked if he had any questions, and asked if he had any family he wanted me to speak to. I went through the whole thing again with his wife that afternoon. I explained that Craig had to cut out all of the smoking, drugs and alcohol, otherwise, although he might never need it, he wouldn't be considered for a heart transplant. They both cried when I mentioned that. Craig thanked me, and shook my hand.

Craig was with us for two weeks on that admission. He got better, lost about twenty kilograms of water, and walked out a new man, in body and I hope, mind as well. After that day, and through the rest of his admission, Craig's racist abuse vanished; he was apologetic, newly respectful to the nurses and the ward staff and generally became the model patient. He even left several Thank You cards and a giant box of Ferrero Rochers when he left. I noticed he'd try to hide his obvious swastika tattoos when we came round, tugging at his shirt sleeve to cover it. I like to think at some point he got it removed, but that might be wishful thinking.

**

I'm often asked how I can deal with patients like Craig, or abusive and rude relatives of patients. Firstly, we are seeing these people on their very worst days: they are sick, they are terrified, they are livid at the thought that their loved one is being neglected. These are not their best selves, nor can we expect them to be. Secondly, we aren't here to befriend them, we are here to make them better. That's the job. Nearly every abusive or racist patient I've ever had doesn't stay that way for long, although with rare exceptions. Those parts of themselves, that anger and frustration and petty hate, disappear like morning mist in the sun when they face something unyielding and real and terrifying, like their own mortality.

**

Whatever we have to deal with; faeces, blood, bodily fluids, the occasional abuse, the stress, it's the messier parts of the job that are also the most humanising. We are pushed outside of everyday society by our constant exposure to the socially unacceptable. The social stigma we attach to biological functions stops at the door of a hospital or GP surgery. Working inside quickly grinds down those sensibilities, leaving a simple truth.

We will all get sick, we all defecate, urinate, vomit. We can all make mistakes. We will all die. Simply, we are all human beings. Fallible, messy, wonderful human beings. It's a unique perspective I am thankful for; despite what we have to deal with to gain it. That being said, I'm also thankful for my poor sense of smell.

Dopamine

It has become commonplace now to hear the mind and the brain described in similar terms to a machine. We are "hardwired", our brains "process" and "store" data. In the collective consciousness of the twenty first century our brains are seen as computers; binary, linear, sensible and logical machines. As apt as it sounds the fact remains this terminology has only really been around for thirty years and that our brains actually behave nothing like the ordered electrical circuits of your iPhone.

At a cellular level the brain is more like a tree, each neuron spreading fine branches to a hundred or a thousand other neurons, each nanometres apart but not quite touching their counterpart. Into that space little puffs of neurohormones are squirted across in response to electrical stimuli, propagating the electrical signal onwards. The more two neurons fire together, the more branch connections are made, and the stronger the signal next time. This is the biological process of learning and memory. A variety of these neurotransmitters slosh around a human brain, including glutamate, serotonin and dopamine.

Dopamine is ubiquitous in the part of the brain once considered to be the seat of emotion, known as the limbic system[32]. From the Latin meaning "border" the limbic system is actually a slim arc of neuronal tissue that straddles the base of both halves of the cortex. From what we understand about it, it's the part of the brain most associated with reward and conditioning. Through release of dopamine across neural junctions behaviour becomes "hardwired". This is not only the biochemical basis for reinforcing good behaviour but also damaging behaviours, like addictions. Far from a moral or lifestyle choice, increasingly we recognise addiction is primarily a disease of the brain. The natural reward system can become corrupted to fire perpetually in response to drugs or alcohol. Worse, the parts of the brain meant to warn you of danger, producing stress and fear responses, become entangled with a lack of those drugs, until you only feel normal or happy when you use, and feel only anxiety and terror when you don't. You are addicted.

---

[32] Di Chiara G, Morelli M, Acquas E, Carboni E. Functions of dopamine in the extrapyramidal and limbic systems. Clues for the mechanism of drug actions. Arzneimittelforschung. 1992 Feb;42(2A):231–7.

Being somewhat oblivious in my first days as a qualified doctor to how stressful and emotionally draining they really were, I didn't pay enough attention to my responses to it. To how much I was starting to drink. It's easy to do: after a hard day, a glass of wine at the door, another with dinner, a second to finish up. That quickly became half a bottle a night, sometimes more. Come payday the pub was full of new doctors commiserating. It was easy to slip into. Your brain has evolved to be highly adaptable, rapidly learning new behaviours and wiring those neurons together so they'll fire more easily next time. This is how you learn to ride a bike. It's also how you can become addicted.

Bill was addicted to alcohol. At 55, he had been bouncing in and out of hospital for nearly a year by the time I met him in my first few months as a doctor, usually drunk, sometimes sick with drinking related illnesses. A few months before he'd landed in the emergency department with a bleed in his stomach, from a knot of blood vessels caused by alcohol damage to his liver. The sluggish blood backing up to such an extent the pressure builds and the vessels rupture.

I'd met Bill on that first admission, recovering on a medical ward, a lanky East Londoner, pepper pot wiry hair, always a couple days of grey beard adorning a wide jaw. I liked Bill. He was genuinely funny, called all the ladies "darling" and all the male staff "fella", always said thank you and did seem genuinely thankful for our care.

Which surprised me. Why did Bill keep drinking? I thought he just didn't understand how sick it was making him. I thought he was making a choice, a foolish one. Each time he was discharged home he'd promise he'd stay dry this time, he'd say his goodbyes to the ward staff and disappear jauntily into the outside world. A few weeks later, back he came. This time he was really sick.

I saw Bill by chance, he was lying on a trolley in the emergency department monitored bay for the very sickest patients called Resuscitation. He looked pale and flat. He gave me a weak smile but I don't think he recognised me. His blood pressure was bleeping ominously above his head, 90/60mmHg.

A voice behind me interjected.

"Are you the surgical F1[33]?" A terse voice, belonging to one of the emergency doctors.

"Um...yes."

"I've just spoken to your senior. That's your next patient." He pointed to Bill, at the same time as his heart rate started to drift slowly upwards. 100, 102, 108.

"Ok... do you know what's wrong with him?" I asked, slightly thrown by this unorthodox referral.

---

[33] F1 is the grade given to doctors in their very first year of practice.

"Pancreatitis." And with that he stuffed his notes in my hands and disappeared back into the chaos of the department.

I knew enough to know that meant the gland in Bill's stomach was inflamed, and that this was a very serious, often deadly condition.

I turned back to Bill, as his blood pressure reading flashed up again. 86/55mmHg. He was getting worse.

**

It has long been acknowledged that our health system and indeed our society does too little for mental health conditions compared to physical ones. In recent years there has been a push for mental health to reach "parity of esteem"[34] with physical health but the resources and staffing have simply not followed. On the other side, alcohol and drug addicted patients are often scapegoated as the "time wasters" and scroungers of the system. The Victorian perception of addiction as a moral defect, not a biological disease, still persists to this day.

Bill had a serious alcohol addiction that was killing him, but that was just a symptom of a greater illness. Bill had started drinking heavily after getting divorced, and then subsequently lost his job, and then his home. From what I gathered when I phoned his next of kin he was living with his mother again, sometimes sleeping rough. He was depressed, addicted and had nowhere to go but down.

**

Slightly more experienced now, I put Bill on a drip, took some blood and brought my registrar and then the consultant round to see him. He was admitted to our surgical ward, and I spent the next eight hours putting up more fluid, taking blood tests and trying to get somebody to come back and see him. His blood pressure just wouldn't stay up. I gave him what seemed like endless bags of fluid, so much I was worried I'd drown him.

Whenever I spoke to someone on the phone he didn't sound too bad. The surgical registrar, the intensive care registrar, my own senior house officer. When they heard the numbers they just reassured me, told me to carry on. 5pm came and went. Bill still looked terrible. I gave him more fluid. 6pm melted into 7pm. My wife now and fiancée at the time, sent a questioning text.

"Everything ok?"

"Not really." I dashed off a reply.

---

[34] Millard C, Wessely S. Parity of esteem between mental and physical health. BMJ [Internet]. 2014 Nov 14 [cited 2020 Feb 12];349.

8pm came round. I just couldn't leave him. Frustrated and stressed and anxious I went and found the night surgical registrar and told him about Bill in person. Natalie was a very senior surgical registrar, very nearly a consultant herself, but she always had time for us junior doctors and was always supportive.

She nodded sagely as I handed Bill's case and story over, exasperated.

"How much fluid did you give him in total?" She asked gently.

I looked down at my scraps of notes, totting it up.

"One and a half litres."

She gave me a knowing grin, and then laughed a bit.

"That's not nearly enough."

**

An inflamed pancreas is a deadly condition. The cascading release of enzymes stored inside makes the pancreas essentially digest itself. The inflammation makes your body lose gallons of fluid into the spaces inside your abdomen[35]. As I know now, some patients can require anywhere north of five litres of fluid just to keep their blood vessels open. Pancreatitis has a high rate of death, and quite often patients can get very sick very fast.

Feeling emotionally and physically exhausted, I trudged home, now also feeling slightly foolish. With no sense of irony at all, I drank a whole bottle of wine and fell asleep.

**

Bill, like so many addicts, had fallen into the gap between mental and physical health. The border between the two is a dangerous place to be. Studies show that patients with a mental health condition do much worse compared to healthy patients when both are afflicted with the same physical condition, and are less likely to receive the same standard of physical care[36]. Bill got better again, and went home with support from alcohol services. I didn't see him come back, and I hope he managed to stay well, but I sadly doubt it.

[35] Aggarwal A, Manrai M, Kochhar R. Fluid resuscitation in acute pancreatitis. World J Gastroenterol. 2014 Dec 28;20(48):18092–103.

[36] DE HERT M, CORRELL CU, BOBES J, CETKOVICH-BAKMAS M, COHEN D, ASAI I, et al. Physical illness in patients with severe mental disorders. I. Prevalence, impact of medications and disparities in health care. World Psychiatry. 2011 Feb;10(1):52–77.

Flash forward six years and as a cardiology registrar I commonly look after patients in limbo between mental and physical health. From experience their care is always challenging. How do you convince a man with paranoid delusions to take his life-saving blood thinning medication when he believes adamantly they are poison? What do you do when the psychoactive medications keeping a woman's severe schizophrenia under control start to actually poison her heart muscle? Mental and physical health issues are incredibly difficult to manage together.

**

Whenever I think about heart conditions in the mentally unwell I always remember Sally.

Sally was in her mid-thirties, straggly blonde hair, dangerously thin and hopelessly addicted to crack cocaine and heroin. Whether drugs had ruined her life or her ruined life led her to drugs it was impossible to tease apart. Probably both. Physically drugs had given her a heart attack, destroyed her heart valve, scarred her lungs, wasted her body, infected her with lifelong and life-threatening viruses. Mentally drugs had pushed her into depression, anxiety and addiction. A psychiatrist had tried to diagnose her with a personality disorder, common with substance abuse, but she'd never been well enough or around often enough to actually be assessed.

I met Sally for the first time on my second ever day as a Cardiology registrar, in the intensive care unit. The night before she'd inhaled cocaine, in a form known as crack. Cocaine, for reference, can be snorted (coke), smoked (crack) or injected. Crack cocaine can be heated with a lighter and a metal spoon or glass pipe, vaporizing at 90 degrees Celsius[37]. When inhaled it hits the bloodstream in 8 seconds, surging into the reward centres and releasing a flood of dopamine. This is the "high" experienced by drug users. Crack cocaine is often mixed with other substances to bulk it out to increase weight and extend profits. Common agents include talc, chalk, potassium permanganate, even other routine medications. Sometimes these substances can be harmless but others can be deadly.

[37] Estroff TW. Manual of Adolescent Substance Abuse Treatment. American Psychiatric Publishing; 2008. 319 p.

Sally had heated up crack cocaine and inhaled it. A mix of cocaine and whatever poison had been cut with it rushed into her alveoli, lining them. Her lungs had attacked the irritant as if they were an infection and filled up with fluid, the tissues so inflamed by the poison now lining them that oxygen simply couldn't get through. High-pressure oxygen had to be pumped into her lungs to keep her alive. Where her chest x-ray should've showed the dark spaces of air-filled lungs and the rib cage of a healthy thirty-five-year-old woman, her lungs were a pair of fluffy white wings, opaque and airless. Her ribs resembled tree roots. Instead of smooth curves, they were gnarled from past fractures, healing into knots of bone. The x-ray told a story of pain, of suffering and addiction.

The intensive care team had asked for cardiology to review, concerned by her extensive heart history. We did a bedside scan and couldn't find anything wrong with her heart to explain her lungs. We handed her care back to the intensive care team. A few days later her lungs had improved and she was discharged.

**

A few months later she returned, with a new problem. By a quirk of geography and my rotations that year Sally came back to a different hospital, and I was still her cardiology doctor. She didn't remember me of course. Sally had been brought in by ambulance that morning, collapsed and feverish at home. Her skin was red hot to touch, and when the admitting medical doctor touched her stethoscope to Sally her heart roared with every beat, a whoosh so loud you could hear it with your own ears if you leaned in close enough. Sally had a new and deadly disease: an infection of her heart.

But it wasn't cocaine this time that was the source of her woes. It was her first and worst addiction: heroin.

Heroin is a derivative of opium; one of the oldest drugs of abuse in human history. Its biochemical structure resembles another natural human neurotransmitter called endorphin, a hormone associated with euphoric joy. In the modern era heroin can be smoked, injected into blood vessels or even into skin known as "skin popping". Each time it's injected it tears and scars the vessel, as well as other parts of the body predisposing to infection the next time. Intravenous drug users eventually run out of veins and develop chronic infections at reused sites that never heal properly.

Sally had injected through one of these sites. When the needle pierced the skin, millions of microbes did too. When she injected these showered into her bloodstream, a deluge of bacteria. They could end up anywhere; in the discs of the spine, as blood clots in the lungs, or stuck to one of the scarred valves of her heart. You only have to be unlucky once to get a potentially lethal infection of the heart.

In her foreshortened life Sally was unlucky three times.

**

The biology of addiction is as tragic as it is fascinating. Dopamine drives neuronal wiring to create a very efficient and very harmful pattern of behaviour that once set is near impossible to break out of. Put bluntly the brain can be quite easily trained to kill you.

As an aside there are conditions where we physically give man-made dopamine to patients for other reasons. In Parkinson's disease the main defect is in a dopamine dependent part of the brain called the substantia nigra.[38] Unable to process movement once this area becomes damaged, patients with Parkinson's rapidly become stiff, slow moving and even frozen without man-made dopamine given as tablets. However, it's an inexact science: the dopamine is absorbed all over the brain, not just to where the defect is. This can lead to a disease called Dopamine dysregulation syndrome[39], where patients start to display impulsive and addictive behaviours; like gambling, shopping, drug abuse and even sex addiction. Some of the case reports make for disturbing reading: a retiree so addicted to online gambling she sold her family home to fund it, becoming homeless. A happily married man of fifty years who became a compulsive sex addict, so addicted to sex he divorced his wife, spent his life savings on prostitutes and carried bags of condoms everywhere he went, including clinic appointments. These patients were left with a terrible choice: give up their mobility and movement, or keep their freedom but lose themselves entirely. Their physical health or their mental health.

For patients like Sally the choice wasn't as black or white. By that point she had no choice at all.

**

Sally survived that admission. Her damaged heart valve flailed inside the left chamber of her heart, its tip and seat eroded by the bacterial infection, but her fevers eventually settled, her blood pressure restored. After six weeks of a thrice-daily cocktail of strong antibiotics, weekly heart scans and a brief stint in intensive care, Sally was well enough to go home.

---

[38] Galvan A, Wichmann T. Pathophysiology of Parkinsonism. Clin Neurophysiol. 2008 Jul;119(7):1459–74.

[39] O'Sullivan SS, Evans AH, Lees AJ. Dopamine dysregulation syndrome: an overview of its epidemiology, mechanisms and management. CNS Drugs. 2009;23(2):157–70.

Being a long stay patient I got to know Sally pretty well. She wasn't a "nice person" by any reasonable definition. She was rude, sometimes abusive, occasionally racist. She'd demand pain medication in the middle of the night, refuse her other medications, complain loudly about the food, the noise, the television. When she was discharged she missed her follow up appointments, and once again became lost in the system.

I'd often get dispatched to assuage Sally's latest tirade, the nurses didn't have the time or the patience to talk her down and in their defence Sally rarely gave them a chance to. Like many similar patients Sally would try and manipulate the staff, swearing blue at the nurses and then swearing blind to the doctors it didn't happen. After ten or fifteen minutes talking Sally would often run out of steam, and I'd catch a glimpse of the person underneath. Sally could be quite charming occasionally, even child-like. In those brief moments, I wondered how Sally had ended up here.

**

After a few months lost in the ether, Sally popped back up, a near rerun of the same symptoms. Fever, collapse, her blood and heart once again flooded with bacteria. She'd continued to use heroin, a path her brain seemed hopelessly hardwired to drag her down endlessly. Again, she had to go back to intensive care. Again, a long stint in hospital on another cocktail of antibiotics.

"You again?" She snorted when she saw me.

"Nice to see you too Sally"

That third admission did seem somewhat different however. Sally had now spent more time in hospitals in that year than she had outside. Something she reflected on when our drugs and alcohol liaison, a specialist link to community care for substance abuse patients, managed to make some headway with her. Sally calmed down on the ward, she wasn't so adversarial and even signed a contract promising not to use drugs, at least not while she was still a patient, and hopefully long term. After three weeks of exemplary behaviour we arranged for her to have a long tube inserted into a large vein so she wouldn't have to continue to endure the multiple (usually failed) attempts at re-siting the temporary tubes we place in short stay patients.

And then, on a cold bright Tuesday afternoon, Sally got suddenly and inexplicably incredibly sick. Weeks after her first illness all her symptoms came crashing back: sky-high fever, plummeting blood pressure and some new ones: chest pain and difficulty breathing. I remember she deteriorated rapidly before our eyes, quite quickly the whole medical emergency team was at her bedside. I couldn't explain what had happened, she hadn't missed any antibiotics, she hadn't been off the ward at all. She'd been getting better.

The portable heart ultrasound or echocardiogram showed the answer. A new clump of infection was now sitting on the other side of her heart, the previously healthy right side, eating away that heart valve until the blood was just a heaving column pumping the wrong way with each beat. A scan of her lungs confirmed it: both lungs were filled with dozens of deposits of bacteria.

It's a common misconception amongst drug users that they need to still use a needle to inject into a medicine line, like the tube we had given Sally the week before. They are designed to be needle free, so the nurses administering just have to connect the tubes. A trick I'd picked up when working in an inner London infection unit; check the line for needle marks. My heart sank when I saw those punctures on Sally's long line. Sally had injected again, this time directly into her heart via the line we had given her.

Going rapidly downhill with no other options left to fix the damage, someone tried to get in touch with Sally's family. Having looked after Sally for months I'd never met any of her kin, so was surprised to sit down an hour later with a well-dressed young lady who introduced herself as Cassie, Sally's daughter.

I started to break the news gently that Sally was very unwell and in mortal danger but Cassie interrupted.

"We know." I remember she had a very calm voice, even though she can't have been more than seventeen, with a slight Scottish lilt. She told me later she'd be raised by her grandmother in Edinburgh. "I've had this chat quite a few times now. Is she dying?"

I paused. I nodded.

"It certainly looks that way. Is she still using?"

"Her partner still is so she probably is too"

A moment of silence. Outside it's any other Tuesday afternoon.

"How did it come to this?"

Cassie relayed some of Sally's life to me. Like so many others in similar situations Sally wasn't really born with a chance. As a child she'd been happy and smart, until a physically abusive father pushed her to run away at thirteen. Abusive relationship after abusive relationship fell into drug abuse and then sexual abuse. Sally had Cassie at fifteen and Cassie was in foster care by the age of three months, with her grandmother at one-years-old. They'd had a loose relationship for all the years after that, not quite mother and daughter. Certainly in Cassie's late teens they had reversed roles. Sally had a few brief spells without drugs, but was too crippled financially and socially to stay sober. Society shunted Sally into her eventual end as much as her brain did. For nearly a decade she'd be in and out of hospitals up and down the country. It was somewhat impressive she'd managed to survive through all of that. But no longer.

Sally passed away later that evening.

**

From personal and professional experience, the resources for mental health care in the community in the UK have been slashed to the bone. The irony of this cost cutting is that it simply costs more to care for these patients further down the line: in crisis situations, in physical beds when they should be in mental health beds, when their physical health becomes an emergency itself, like with Sally. We don't seem to be able to manage mental health care nearly as well as we should, a crisis brewing without signs of being addressed. All the while that continues unabated, patients will suffer and die. Patients like Sally.

Microbe

Sally ultimately died of her addiction, but her final disease was simply the wrong bacteria in the wrong place at the wrong time. You might think of bacteria as interlopers, singular intruders amongst your human cells. In fact, it's quite the opposite. The largest part of you that makes up you isn't actually you at all. From an alien perspective, an external scan of your body would show a complex organism made up of trillions of cells, with up to 90% of those cells being bacteria[40].

Which may be hard to swallow, figuratively and literally. Despite extensively studying bacteria, disease and antibiotics for centuries we still don't know very much about this hidden microbiological world, especially inside our own bodies. The human body, particularly skin, stomach, intestines and colon, are literally covered in a whole ecosystem of bugs, many of which we are yet to name or even successfully isolate.

Not all bacteria cause disease, quite the opposite. Many of them serve a useful purpose, perhaps even more useful than we realise. Occasionally one bacteria can run rampant in the bowel, overgrowing everything else and starting to cause symptoms like diarrhoea, fever and pain. This is *Clostridium Difficile* infection, which can become deeply entrenched and nearly intractable to treatment. It comes about when antibiotics kill off much of the rest of the bowel flora, and *Difficult* grows rapidly across the space left behind like a weed. The natural diversity of bugs in the bowel protects your gut from both external and also internal infections.
Occasionally antibiotics alone cannot make a *C. Difficile* infection better and the only option is a revolutionary method to replace your bowel flora, essentially give you back the entire bacterial garden that the *C. Difficile* grew over. How? Well your particular blend of bowel bacteria is passed down to you from your mother and family in early childhood. So the very simple but very odd procedure is a transplant. Of faeces. From a close relative. Yes, it's as weird as it sounds.[41]

---

[40] NIH Human Microbiome Project defines normal bacterial makeup of the body [Internet]. National Institutes of Health (NIH). 2015 [cited 2020 Feb 12].

[41] Quraishi MN, Widlak M, Bhala N, Moore D, Price M, Sharma N, et al. Systematic review with meta-analysis: the efficacy of faecal microbiota transplantation for the treatment of recurrent and refractory Clostridium difficile infection. Aliment Pharmacol Ther. 2017;46(5):479–93.

A suspension of a family member's faeces is created and then passed into the patient via a long tube directly into the small bowel or sometimes as a frozen capsule.

This can cure chronic C. *Difficile* infection but has had some unintended side effects. In 2010 a US mother who received a faecal transplant from her obese daughter was cured of the infection, but after a few months rapidly gained weight, becoming obese herself.[42] The researchers concluded that your bowel bacteria may play a pivotal role in the metabolism of food and regulation of body weight. Further research might prove to be ground-breaking in our understanding of obesity.

All of which is to say that bacteria are like people; in the wrong place at the wrong time they could do a lot of damage, but they aren't all malevolent. Please bear that in mind.

**

It's 2013 and I am finishing up my first year as a doctor in the microbiology laboratory. This is where all the samples to look for bacteria are received and processed; in urine, faeces, blood, skin swabs and all manner of biopsies and extracted fluids. Samples can be grown in an incubator and looked at under microscopes, stained with various dyes or even ionised into individual atoms and then accelerated in a machine called a mass spectrometer to identify which bacteria are present. The information generated here has huge implications for the patient's these samples come from.

As a doctor it's a rare insight into the hospital activity off the ward: I have an office in the laboratory, and spend portions of my day staring down microscopes at tiny flagellating microbes. It's a hot day in July, and I'm just about done, halfway to the door when I pass Dr Langley's office.

Dr Langley is the senior microbiology consultant here, and has worked in this department longer than I've been alive, longer than my parents have been married. Despite his lanky six four frame, he is incredibly softly spoken. He whispers to me in his comically proper RP[43] accent.

"Dominic, my boy, come here one second."

I dutifully follow him into his office. He gestures at a 90's black and green computer display with a few lines of text flashing gently. Despite the high-tech machines we have, I still can't believe how dated some of the lab software is. "What do you make of this?"

---

[42] Alang N, Kelly CR. Weight Gain After Fecal Microbiota Transplantation. Open Forum Infect Dis [Internet]. 2015 Feb 1 [cited 2020 Feb 12];2(1). Available from: https://www.ncbi.nlm.nih.gov/pmc/articles/PMC4438885/

[43] RP - received pronunciation accent, a 'formal' British accent associated with early television and radio broadcast on the BBC.

Slightly perplexed at what could be so intriguing about three lines of MS DOS text I scrutinise them. It's a readout for a bacteria culture - the lab has grown bacteria from a patient's tissue sample and have tested it against various antibiotics to see which one can treat it.

Next to every single line it says a single word: RESISTANT.

I scroll to the next page. Every antibiotic they've tested against this strain of bacteria: RESISTANT. The next page is the same. I scroll back, checking each antibiotic. It's resistant to all of them, all the antibiotics we have. All the antibiotics that exist.

Dr Langley sees I've understood.

"Luckily this is just a skin sample, the patient is very well."

"What would happen if someone became unwell with this?" I ask, genuinely frightened. I've never seen a readout like this before.

"Well my boy, this might be what ends humanity. The 'Apocalypse Bug' " exclaims Dr Langley, his eyes just slightly too wide.

Despite the boiling July weather, I shiver.

**

It's the middle of February, four years later, and I'm working in an Intensive Care unit in the middle of London. I'm staring down at a paper printout, getting that same chill down my spine that I felt all those years ago. This is the paperwork for the gentleman that's just been flown in from Greece. Georgios is a fifty-two-year-old businessman; in the last year he's travelled all over Europe and Asia buying and selling parts for farming machinery. Somewhere between Singapore and Athens he started feeling feverish, sweaty, with a constant hacking cough. After a few days feeling terrible, he went and found a family doctor in the middle of Athens, who admitted him straight to their hospital, where he'd spiralled downwards, needing heart pumping medication, tubes for his breathing and for his kidneys. Every organ was failing. They took samples for infection and found this. The paper I'm staring at. The reason he was sent back to the UK and now into our double secure isolation room, the room we drilled to use in the event of an Ebola outbreak.

The hospital name is in Greek, but the results below are perfect English. I see lines and lines of the word: RESISTANT. Georgios has, as Dr Langley put it, the "Apocalypse Bug". He has an infection we have no ability to treat, and he is dying.

**

Antibiotic resistance is one of the biggest threats to humanity in the view of many in the medical community. More than nuclear war and second only to climate change, the rise of infections we have no treatments for threatens our entire way of life. If that seems an exaggeration you only have to look at a time before antibiotics to understand how cheap life was then.

Prior to Alexander Fleming discovering that extracts from certain moulds would prevent the growth of bacteria, thus discovering penicillin, life was very different. Infection was a spectre that stalked society, striking indiscriminately. Pneumonia was common and deadly, tuberculosis or leprosy was treated by forced imprisonment in a sanatorium or leprosarium respectively, rampant syphilis ate through a patient's blood vessels, brain tissue and even nose. Any surgical operation whatsoever was nearly impossible without killing the majority of patients. Periodic outbreaks would wipe out entire generations: more people died of Spanish influenza in 1918 than were killed in conflict in World War 1[44]. Cholera, plague, Scarlet fever, measles; the Grim Reaper's scythe swung wide and low and often.

The invention of penicillin kick-started a new era, and alongside industrialisation, vaccination and societal welfare programmes, the devastation of infectious diseases receded into the shadows. Modern medicine is utterly dependent on being able to fight and control microbes. Without antibiotics, we wouldn't be able to give chemotherapy or perform surgery. Childbirth and pregnancy would be a deadly minefield of potential infections. It's remarkable we live in such a sanitised society where this isn't immediately obvious.

---

[44] 1918 Pandemic (H1N1 virus) | Pandemic Influenza (Flu) | CDC [Internet]. 2019 [cited 2020 Feb 12]. Available from: https://www.cdc.gov/flu/pandemic-resources/1918-pandemic-h1n1.html

That's not to say it's been smooth sailing or indeed a total triumph. No one anticipated in the fight against infectious diseases the microbes would fight back. The ability of microbes to develop cellular defences against antibiotics is termed "resistance". Resistance comes about when strains of bacteria develop random mutations that nullify the effect of an antibiotic. This by itself isn't necessarily a problem; like C. *Difficile* the biggest barrier to bacteria growth and causing illness is other bacteria. Even if single bacteria becomes resistant to antibiotics it still has to out-compete the other strains to become a colony large enough to cause disease. But if you apply too many antibiotics, killing off all the non-resistant strains, those bacteria with their protective mutations will flourish, and then cause illness and spread to other people. This is how resistance arises in communities. It's estimated that resistant bacteria kill around 100,000 people in the US every year[45].

The overuse of antibiotics and expectations of being given antibiotics are problems on both sides of the doctor patient relationship. The concept of appropriate limitation of antibiotics is vital to responsible prescribing, protecting the community as a whole. We even had an exam station at my medical school addressing this exact issue. An actress plays the role of a businesswoman with a sore throat. She attends your GP practice demanding antibiotics to treat her. We know the majority of sore throats are caused by simple viruses, these are self-resolving and are not treated in any way by antibiotics, where they would only cause side effects and increase resistance. So the station is half clinical assessment and half conflict resolution: the patient believes she must have antibiotics, the doctor has to navigate that and still treat the patient properly.

[45] Aslam B, Wang W, Arshad MI, Khurshid M, Muzammil S, Rasool MH, et al. Antibiotic resistance: a rundown of a global crisis. Infect Drug Resist. 2018 Oct 10;11:1645–58.

Unfortunately, this stewardship of antibiotics is not quite as regimented around the world. Super resistant strains of gonorrhoea[46] are on the rise globally, and proving fatal in some cases. Tuberculosis has never really left humanity, but due to profligate use of antibiotics drug resistant and even super drug resistant strains are on the rise, wiping out whole villages in South Africa and Asia[47]. This worldwide shortage of effective antibiotics has been met with a somewhat lukewarm approach from the drug industry. New patents for new drugs are supposed to be fast tracked through development, but in reality the same drugs are being recycled with subtle tweaks, and no new antibiotics are arriving anytime soon. Which means more and more we will be seeing patients like Georgious.

**

It was a strange and sobering experience looking after Georgious. Like my counterparts a hundred years ago, we had no real treatment for his infection. Unlike my counterparts we could keep his heart beating, kidneys working and blood vessels squeezed sufficiently to keep him alive way beyond the point he would've died in the 1900s. And so we did and we just watched. It's a rather odd thought to someone so entrenched in medicine to think someone so sick can get better without any treatment. But if the last six thousand years of civilised human history were a single day, antibiotics only arrived about twenty minutes ago, life support machines about ten minutes ago. Human beings have been fighting infections for millennia. Admittedly often losing, but of course we have a highly adapted immune system for a reason that keeps hundreds of infections at bay every single day.

Georgious was young by our standards at least, and previously well. It was touch and go for a few days but he slowly recovered. After four weeks in the intensive care unit he was fit enough to go home. As he walked through the doors, hugely relieved as we were all were that he'd made it, I couldn't help but think of Georgious as the first of many more to come.

**

---

[46] Unemo M, Shafer WM. Antimicrobial Resistance in Neisseria gonorrhoeae in the 21st Century: Past, Evolution, and Future. Clin Microbiol Rev. 2014 Jul;27(3):587-613.

[47] Prasad R, Singh A, Balasubramanian V, Gupta N. Extensively drug-resistant tuberculosis in India: Current evidence on diagnosis & management. Indian J Med Res. 2017 Mar;145(3):271-93.

Antibiotic resistance threatens to take us back to the Dark Ages of medicine. A crack in the edifice of modern medicine that imperils the entire planet. So the next time the doctor won't prescribe antibiotics for your sore throat, don't be disheartened. You are in fact helping to save the world.

Pineal

It's 0300am. My bleep is mercifully quiet on the table in front of me, lying next to a polystyrene cup of watery hot chocolate and half a NutriGrain bar. Lunch on a busy night shift. My feet ache from criss-crossing the hospital on a twilight safari of blood taking, prescribing medications, inserting cannulas and seeing unwell patients. My bleep vibrates noisily against the wooden table and I sleepily dial the extension.

"Drug chart please doctor"

I just mumble something sleepily and hang up. I brush the crumbs off my scrubs and trudge back out into the corridors.

I stop.

Forty yards in front of me is a scraggly red-brown fox. In the hospital corridor. He's frozen mid-stride, a forepaw hovering in the air, perfectly still.

I'm not sure if I'm hallucinating, I'm on my second night of four and my body clock is still struggling with the day-night cycle crossover. Scrawny, ruddy brown fur, he looks at me balefully with tired orange eyes. For a beat neither of us move. My breath mists in front of me, it's the middle of winter. With a flick of his head the fox trots off, down a side corridor and out into the night.

I'm alone again. Still not a hundred percent sure that actually happened, I trot off in my own direction back into the deserted bowels of a hospital at night.

**

I don't believe in ghosts, for the simple reason thousands of patients die every year in hospital, yet I've spent hundreds of hours of night shifts there and never once felt the ethereal presence of a restless soul. Even working in the very oldest and gothic hospital buildings, sometimes wandering into the medieval chapel at 0200am to play the piano when no one is around, I've always felt completely and oddly comfortable alone on a night shift.

After-hours in a hospital feels very much like stepping into a parallel dimension; into the Upside Down, all of the buildings and beds and rooms are the same, but everything else is different. It's darker, for obvious reasons, and we often go to gloomy bedsides to examine patients, a single pool of lamplight to see by, whispering so as not to try and wake the patient next door. There's also far less people, most of the routine everyday activity of the hospital finishes in the evening; outpatient appointments and day surgery, clerical work and routine scans all work 9-5 for the most part, and rightly so. The cost of asking the secretaries to work night shifts would be as prohibitive as it would be unnecessary. The absence of the buzz of patient and visitor activity is eerie, empty lifts, deserted lobbies, vacant and closed cafeterias. The night shift is reduced to core staff; doctors, nurses and midwives plus on-call radiographers and physiotherapists, porters, lab technicians and security. It's quite common to traipse across a hospital at midnight and not see a soul. It's actually quite unnerving to see anyone at all. The wards are sleeping and for the staff it feels most akin to being on an overnight flight. There's a quiet activity that's never quite silent, a dark that's never quite complete.

Generally, I used to quite like nights. For one thing it's a pure emergency service, which means lots of the administrative clutter of the day to day such as outpatient referrals, GP letters and box ticking of routine tests, all disappear. It's pure medicine, pure patient need. It feels like what being a doctor should be like all of the time. Especially as overnight you deal with emergencies often alone, with your team elsewhere in the hospital on the end of a phone or a bleep. It's rare that I've felt unsupported and I have certainly learnt more about being a doctor and about myself in those moments of decision making at night than during the day.

That's not to say night shifts are easy, far from it.

**

It's 9pm on a summer night in 2014 and I am a middle grade doctor in a busy London hospital. Each night shift begins with a huddle of all the members of the Hospital at Night Team; the roving band of doctors and nurses that will crew the hospital on to the morning. Overnight the ship is captained by the Medical Registrar, a senior training doctor a few years from consultancy. The day team are twiddling their thumbs waiting to go home. The night team is keen to get on. The clock ticks past 9.10.

For reasons still unfathomable to me now, a gigantic cuddly toy dog sits smiling goofily in one corner, holding a pink card that reads "Thank you so much". Presumably for the ward, it has been dumped unceremoniously in the handover room. As a joke I take the dog and sit it in the empty night registrar's seat.

"Ready to go!"

The room gives a light chuckle, but we continue to wait, and the humour quickly fades into thumb chewing nervousness. The clock comes up to 9.25. We are calling to find out where the Night Medical Registrar is. The ship has no captain. The toy dog smiles ominously in their empty chair.

**

It's not uncommon to suddenly have to fill a more senior role, or "acting up" as we term it. It's actually encouraged at a certain level of training and in a supervised manner. None of this means much to me as the decision comes down to give me the wheel of the ship, about two years too early, when it seems like the Medical Registrar that fateful night was destined to be a no show.

I hold the bleep fearfully, knowing on the other end will be the emergency department with new patients, the medical wards with very unwell patients, the obstetric ward with terrifying patients. I don't listen much to the meeting as it rolls on, chanting a silent prayer to myself.

"Please don't be busy. Please don't be busy."

It's busy.

The bleep goes off once. It's the ED. "We have a really unwell gentleman, he's struggling to breath despite high-flow oxygen, he's 23 and he just got off a flight from Dubai."

"Sure." I say weakly. "We will see."

The bleep goes off again. A&E once more. "Hi, DKA in resus 3. Thanks." Phone goes dead. I know DKA means diabetic ketoacidosis, a life-threatening emergency in diabetic patients. I also know with me acting up we are short a team member to see both patients. I ask one of the other juniors to come down and I'll supervise them while seeing the young man. The bleep goes off again. And again. And again.

Come midnight I'm hovering once again in the sickest area of A&E; Resuscitation, flitting back and forth between three very unwell patients like a hummingbird while fielding phone calls from everywhere in the hospital. My young patient from Dubai is getting worse and now going to intensive care. I don't know what's wrong with him but to my credit two consultants don't know either. I suggested he might have a virus from the Middle East called MERS, so he's going to a quarantine bed upstairs. My other patients are okay for now but I'm so frantic I can't help but keep checking on them in between other things.

At around 12.30 the real night registrar turns up. Due to a mix up with the rota he wasn't scheduled for tonight and has driven back from Kent. He takes the bleep back from my shaky hands and then we walk around the patients. He makes quick clear decisions that set the patients on the right path. I'm secretly pleased and relieved he mostly doesn't change anything I had done.

The night waxed and waned toward morning and when the sun came up I found five minutes to sit outside the hospital and watch the sun rise over the heart of central London. I sat outside in the crisp morning air, still in my scrubs and beat-up trainers, watching the morning commuter crowd stream by. I felt like an interloper freshly returned to the real world from a twilight one. I was unscathed and so were my patients. Grinning to myself at 6am in the cool dawn air, I felt triumphant. Sometimes in this job it's enough just to survive.

**

Not every night shift is like that one. I've covered busier and far quieter shifts. Christmas Eve is usually very quiet, those sick at home trying to cling on to make it to Christmas Dinner. Christmas Night on the other hand is usually very busy, as those unwell patients who made it through Christmas Day can hold on no longer.

This might seem counter-intuitive. It is often claimed that "patients get sick 24 hours a day, seven days a week", but this isn't really true. Human disease and when human beings get unwell is dependent as much on human behaviour as their actual affliction. If you've ever sat in any A&E you will have seen this, at least until recently.

0800am and most departments used to be deserted. Slowly over the period of the day and then the early evening activity ramps up, to a peak just after 6pm which tapers down again at around 10pm. Monday is the busiest day of the week in A&E, Tuesday is the second busiest[48]. The quietest time if you want to be seen quickly by the way is 5am on Wednesday morning. Even major world events have a significant impact on patient's health. In a German study[49] heart attacks were three times more likely in men whenever Germany played a match in the World Cup compared to non-match days, and twice as likely in women.

---

[48] Statistics » A&E Attendances and Emergency Admissions [Internet]. [cited 2020 Feb 12].

[49] Wilbert-Lampen U, Leistner D, Greven S, Pohl T, Sper S, Völker C, et al. Cardiovascular events during World Cup soccer. N Engl J Med. 2008 Jan 31;358(5):475–83.

Why is this? Firstly, most human diseases are an interaction between some sort of pathogen and human behaviour. Eating out and food poisoning, heart attacks and stressful world cups, drink driving and car accidents, smoking and lung cancer. What we do has a great impact on our health and vice versa. This means that all disease to some extent is influenced by human behaviours, and nothing is more human than the structure of a day or a week.

Secondly, how and when people seek medical attention occurs on a spectrum based on individual personality and choices. For example, the stoic pensioner who never "wanted to trouble anyone" has to be pushed into the emergency department rip-roaringly sick before he'll see a doctor. On the contrary, the anxious twenty something medical student with a little bit of knowledge becomes a hypochondriac with a handbook and is in the ED with a mild headache they are worried is an internal bleed or a brain tumour or something worse and more obscure. Again, this isn't really news to anybody.

Thirdly the availability of healthcare at certain junctures will also determine how patients interact with it. Many will hold out the weekend to see the GP on Monday rather than go to an out of hours service, many will come to A&E after work or after a day of "seeing how it goes" before relenting in the evening.

This predicts very accurately not only how and when patients will come in but also what type of patients come in at what times. Only the most unwell patients come in at any time, so when healthier patients who can choose to not to come in, don't, for example 5am on a Wednesday, a smaller number of people will attend hospital who don't have a choice because they are so unwell. This is exactly what happens on the weekend for example.

All of this is however slightly historical. Since 2010 activity in UK emergency departments has been increasing steadily alongside increasing pressures on social care at the other end of the hospital to discharge patients. This has created a tighter and tighter bottleneck, meaning patients back up into the ED and out of the door. So those "quiet" periods of admission are often now full departments struggling to find beds for the patients who already came in. The number of patients seen, assessed and discharged or admitted within four hours has steadily fallen over the past three years, leaving more and more people stuck in the ED. Since 2010 those waiting over four hours to be assessed and treated has tripled, those stuck on trolleys waiting for a hospital bed over four hours has quintupled. As I'm writing this it's the middle of the hottest July in decades and the hospital is calling an emergency bed crisis meeting. It's always winter now.

All of which is to say intermittently you might find night shifts with prolonged lulls in activity, where a well-timed rest is essential to safely managing to care for patients. Sleep deprivation after one or more missed night's sleep has as harmful a cumulative effect on your decision making, response times and prioritisation skills as alcohol.[50] In other words, after two nights of missed sleep your brain is drunk.

Sleep is incredibly important to professionals working nights. Imagine an airline pilot flying long haul, trying to land a plane without any rest after twelve hours. Would you fly on that airline? It might surprise you to know that many hospitals actively try to stop doctors and nurses having sleep breaks on night shifts, removing on-call rooms and spaces to sleep. Even when it's permitted, many hospitals don't have actual areas for doctors to sleep in.

I've slept in all sorts of funny places on night shifts: bariatric outpatient clinic rooms (the chairs for the morbidly obese are amazingly comfortable), the intensive care device repair room, an overly large window sill, balanced between two wheelie office chairs. Sometimes I've taken night breaks without sleeping: sneaking in to the hospital chapel to play the piano at 2am like the Phantom of the Opera, writing my blog at the ward reception desk in the super-comfy clerk's chair. Being an on-call service you can't really give your bleep to anyone else, so you have to rest with it on your chest or near your head so it'll wake you. Which doesn't sound particularly healthy or safe but that is the reality of nights; there aren't enough staff day or night and no more are coming anytime soon.

We understand we all need sleep. We still don't really understand why. The sleep-wake cycle involves multiple parts of the brain including a small nub of neuronal tissue deep in the very centre of the cerebral cortex; the pineal gland[51]. Descartes believed the pineal gland was the link between the physical brain and the spiritual soul. Even today the pineal gland is still believed by some to be the "Third Eye" or "Anja Chakra", the doorway to unlocking the psychic potential of man. I don't know if there is any medical evidence to support that. However, what we do know about the pineal gland is that it serves a key function in regulating sleep, in marshalling the hormonal responses to daylight and darkness that allow us to sleep at all.[52]

---

50 Killgore WDS. Effects of sleep deprivation on cognition. Prog Brain Res. 2010;185:105–29.

51 Aulinas A. Physiology of the Pineal Gland and Melatonin. In: Feingold KR, Anawalt B, Boyce A, Chrousos G, Dungan K, Grossman A, et al., editors. Endotext [Internet]. South Dartmouth (MA): MDText.com, Inc.; 2000 [cited 2020 Feb 16]. Available from: http://www.ncbi.nlm.nih.gov/books/NBK550972/

52 Masters A, Pandi-Perumal SR, Seixas A, Girardin J-L, McFarlane SI. Melatonin, the Hormone of Darkness: From Sleep Promotion to Ebola Treatment. Brain Disord Ther [Internet]. 2014 [cited 2020 Feb 16];4(1).

We know the extreme effects of not sleeping. The world-record for staying awake was set in 1965 by a American high school student for a school science fair: he managed 11 days[53], and seemed to suffer no ill effects. In animal studies of sleep deprivation rats could be kept awake for around two weeks before they died.[54] Of what exactly we aren't clear, but the outcome was plain; brains need sleep.

**

It's 2015 and I'm working nights on a neurology rotation in one of the country's largest and most well-known neurology hospitals. The ward is quiet, the nurses are doing their paperwork by lamplight at their station and I'm wandering the wards picking up any remaining jobs for the night. It's around 2.30am. I walk past a young man in his thirties, sat bolt upright in his bed, staring around at the ward. He looks at me silently as I pass. His spectre is unnerving in the gloom of the bay, with all of the other patients deeply asleep around him.
I ask the nurses about him.
"Is he okay? Perhaps he needs a sleeping tablet?"
"Anthony?"
I nod, glancing back at his bed. Anthony is simply looking around the ward, silently, without expression.
The nurse just shakes her head sadly.
"He never sleeps."
"Oh. Really? Since when?"
The nurse gives me a hard stare, as if I'm making a crude joke. Her answer jolts me.
"Since April."

**

[53] Ross JJ. NEUROLOGICAL FINDINGS AFTER PROLONGED SLEEP DEPRIVATION. Arch Neurol. 1965 Apr;12:399–403.

[54] Everson CA, Bergmann BM, Rechtschaffen A. Sleep deprivation in the rat: III. Total sleep deprivation. Sleep. 1989 Feb;12(1):13–21.

Anthony was a second generation Italian banker, raised in a poor city borough he had excelled at school and propelled through an economics degree straight into a top job at one of the world's most prestigious hedge funds. Anthony had just bought a flat with his new wife and departed for his honeymoon. He really had everything going for him. On his last night in Mauritius he'd slept soundly and solidly, and woken up to the susurration of the waves on the white sandy beach. That was the last time he ever slept for a significant period of time. A few weeks later he stopped sleeping altogether.

At first he had thought it was the stress of work, of moving, but then his brain began to show signs of damage; his grasp of numbers began to slip, his hands became clumsy and would jerk unexpectedly, he'd struggle to find and form words. After a week of no sleep at all he saw a neurologist, who referred him to a specialist neurologist, who had referred him to here. It took a long time to diagnose Anthony. During that time, I watched him slowly slip away, from a bright and chatty thirty-three-year-old man he stopped speaking, couldn't walk, couldn't do anything unaided.

The diagnosis came back and it was the worst possible news. It had always been unfortunately hopeless. Anthony had Fatal Familial Insomnia (FFI), a disease so rare most doctors will never see a case in two lifetimes. FFI is a genetic condition in the same family as Mad Cow Disease.[55] Strings of misfolded proteins called prions produced in the brain deform normal functioning brain protein into becoming malfunctioning prions themselves, which go on to deform others. Like a virus these prions propagate, progressively destroying brain cell function in an unrelenting march that begins with a patient losing the ability to sleep and invariably ends with dementia, hallucinations and eventually their tragic death.

I became involved in Anthony's case, I met his new wife and his mother, I helped to arrange his eventual hospice care. It's rare to have ever felt so helpless in modern medicine. We could know what was wrong with him but not how to help. We had no treatment. Our understanding of his condition is as limited as our understanding of sleep itself. Perhaps the secrets to both will come with time, but too late for Anthony and the handful of cases like him across the world each year.

**

Night shifts can be mentally, physically and emotionally taxing. The singular pressure of simply shouldering the hospital for a night or four is exhausting. I used to love nights purely for the exhilaration of when they stopped: the post-nights' day.

---

[55] Geschwind MD. Prion Diseases. Continuum (Minneap Minn). 2015 Dec;21(6 Neuroinfectious Disease):1612-38.

Traditionally the Night team should all go for breakfast, these are one of the "rules". It's not any type of normal breakfast however, as your body tells you it's Friday night, not Monday morning. It's hard to know what to eat and what to do in those circumstances but here's my tried and tested post-nights' plan.

First the food; steak and eggs, side order of grits (hot fried diced potato), hot chocolate with a shot of whiskey (if you go somewhere good). Sometimes waffles for after.[56]

Then the day is yours. You have to reset your sleep wake cycle and the best way I've found is to simply stay up till the next night, and fall down exhausted. I map the day out usually the same way each time; read a freshly bought fiction paperback over a coffee, have lunch somewhere unhealthy but nice and cap it off with an afternoon in the cinema.

Which sounds very odd. Why would you go to the cinema, alone, shattered after a twelve-hour night shift and a long morning? To that I say try it. The sleep deprived mind is extremely emotionally labile, like being drunk or febrile your brain's inhibitory shutters roll back and your mind runs deliriously free. The best movie I ever saw in my life was Spider-Man 2, straight after a seven-day stretch of night shifts. I laughed, I cried, I audibly gasped. It was without a doubt the best film I've ever seen. Now I'm not saying that Spider-Man 2 is an Oscar-winning ground-breaking movie. I know this because I've watched it again since, and it's not even particularly good. Which confused me. How can I misremember this as a monumental moment in cinema, when the reality is so drastically different? And if my judgement is so off about this, what else might it be off about?

**

The fatigue-addled mind is fallible, and worse, blind to its failings. I've read written notes from late into my night shifts and spotted missing words, whole sentences that don't go anywhere, entries that aren't finished. I don't recall any of these errors at the time. This is why it's so crucial to be able to rest overnight. The alternatives don't bear thinking about.

A recent report found nearly half of 1,100 doctors surveyed have fallen asleep at the wheel of a car when driving home.[57] Several doctors and nurses have died at the wheel following arduous night shifts. We all understand how important sleep is, but we aren't doing nearly enough to protect our professionals at night, and by extension, to protect the patients under their care.

---

[56] (You can quite quickly see how this makes you very fat if you do this twice a month).

[57] Tired doctors 'fall asleep driving' [Internet]. BBC News. [cited 2020 Feb 13].

Mitosis

I remember the darkest time in my medical career literally and figuratively as endless night. At the close and turn of the year the days get so short long day shifts see you going in and coming out of work in darkness, and night shifts are the only time you catch a glimpse of the sun on your way to sleep.

It's January 2016, I'm sitting on the tube, headed to my third night shift in a set of four working on a cancer intensive care unit. The average age of my patients tonight is twenty-two. One is too young to drive, another too young to drink. All are hopelessly and desperately sick. Each night I sit in handover, numbly listening to their stories and their lists of parameters and their names. Eloise, Jack, Annie. They all sound so young. I'm taking the work home with me and I can't even work out why. I'll snap at my wife, sit for hours in a depressive stupor then throw myself into something obsessively. I sit on the tube and for thirty minutes tears just stream down my face. I get off and go to the next handover. I can't do this for much longer.

**

When people talk about a "cure for cancer" I always find that a peculiar question, like asking "is there a cure for illness?" The popular belief of "cancer" as a single disease to "have" and to "fight" isn't the reality. In truth there are probably as many different cancers as there are people, everyone is treated in very different ways and may have vastly different outcomes. If you want to understand why, you have to look at where cancer comes from.

Einstein is famously quoted as rejecting the randomness of the subatomic world, stating "God doesn't play dice."[58] On a cellular level that is and isn't true. Every cell in your body with some notable exceptions is in a constant state of renewal: your cells divide, multiply and die constantly. If they didn't you wouldn't heal or grow. The process of cellular division involves the replication and division of all of the parts of the cell, including the DNA. Mitosis is the orchestrated sequence of copying the DNA and dividing the two copies into two new cells, which happens in each of us tens of billions of times a day.

The process isn't perfect however. In all of those tens of billions of copies mistakes will have crept in. Although the human genome is approximately three billion "letters" long[59], it is written with just four different amino acids, in two pairs. Like binary code in computers the alternating sequence of just these amino acid pairs contains enough information to weave an entire human being. With each cell division an amino acid may be accidentally swapped or moved or cut or skipped, all of which disrupt the code. There's a whole sub-cellular apparatus dedicated to just correcting these mistakes but it too is fallible.

Each mistake or mutation has the potential to change the function of the cell, although only an infinitesimal number ever do. However, tens of billions mistakes a day, every day, for a lifetime, means that one random cellular change, or rather two or three or more, that could lead to a cancer are very likely. We know the odds from simply counting all the cases of cancer we find. One in two people born after 1960 will be diagnosed with some sort of cancer in their lifetime[60]. There is a lot you can do to modify your risks of cancer, but those fateful dice are written into our DNA. Cancer rates are climbing, in part due to better diagnosis and screening and in part due to populations simply living longer. Like any machine, the probability of breakdown is not a matter of if, but when.

[58] Natarajan V. What Einstein meant when he said 'God does not play dice ...' arXiv:13011656 [physics] [Internet]. 2013 Jan 5 [cited 2020 Feb 13];

[59] Piovesan A, Pelleri MC, Antonaros F, Strippoli P, Caracausi M, Vitale L. On the length, weight and GC content of the human genome. BMC Research Notes. 2019 Feb 27;12(1):106.

[60] Ahmad AS, Ormiston-Smith N, Sasieni PD. Trends in the lifetime risk of developing cancer in Great Britain: comparison of risk for those born from 1930 to 1960. British Journal of Cancer. 2015 Mar;112(5):943-7.

Some of us have the die stacked against us from the moment we are born, carrying genes already predisposed to create cancer cells. Rather than several mistakes, these patients only require one before a cancer is created, and so it manifests far sooner. Given the random nature of most cancers it's unsurprising that it can appear in nearly any organ. By its very nature of starting from a mistake in the genes of a specialised cell each cancer is unique to that tissue but also to that person. This is why cancer is not a single disease any more than the human race is a single person - it's a disease of our natural genetic mechanisms and essentially random. It's the enemy inside the gates, a biological betrayal. It can affect any organ at any time, although statistically some cancers arise much more commonly than others. By its very nature it tends to be a disease of the middle aged and elderly, but not always.

**

After handover we divide into the wings of the unit to round our own cohort of patients. Due to a quirk of the rota I am always covering the West side where we only have individual side rooms, which means complex long stay patients at high risk of infection, which usually means tragically young and terribly sick cancer patients.

Being a night shift the unit is quiet, the hum and click of machines the only background noise. There are no visiting teams or routine operations happening, not much transfers in and out, the activity of the day is stripped back to the necessity of the night: making sure each of these patients will make it through to the morning. As hard as we try it's not always possible.

My first stop this evening is Eloise, a 15-year-old girl thirty days after a stem cell transplant for an aggressive leukaemia. The treatment involves harvesting a donor's healthy infection-fighting white cells, giving radiotherapy and chemotherapy to kill all the cancer cells in the patient and then trying to give the donor cells back to her. It's a very high risk intervention, but for some their only chance at life. For Eloise it would seem she isn't responding, her blood counts aren't rising and she has had infection after infection. A few days prior she'd become unable to breathe independently and she is now back on life support. Hugely swollen from liver and nutritional failure she has become unrecognisable. She seems settled when I enter. Her mother has entrenched herself in one corner, a watchful spectre she barely interacts with us any more herself. What internal hell she is going through I can't begin to contemplate. As Eloise gets slowly worse and worse I begin to feel her mother's presence at the bedside is becoming a vigil. I do the routine things the best I can and murmur something reassuring. Her mother just nods a fraction. It's not enough.

I move on. Sometimes, the treatment for these terrible cancers can be as bad as the disease. My next stop is Sami, a nineteen-year-old boy who had a terrible reaction to his lymphoma treatment. While his disease had been pushed into the recesses for now, the chemotherapy had had a very rare but devastating side effect, leaving him with brain damage, intractable seizures and unable to communicate or interact meaningfully. He was sleeping peacefully, mercifully seizure free for a few hours. His father wasn't there: Sami had been in the hospital so long now his family had arranged their own room to stay in overnight a few minutes away. Little to do, I move on.

Next door, Jessica is too young to drive or vote, and never will. She has an aggressive lymphoma, no immune system left and is awash with a myriad of fungal and bacterial infections. She is in a condition beyond critical. Her heart had already stopped beating twice over the last two nights, each time we had just about brought her back, but only just.

In the morning the team had decided to stop trying to resuscitate her. The worst conversation I can ever imagine having to discuss as a patient or a parent or a doctor. Her own parents had left not ten minutes before. When I enter, her nurse is looking concerned. As with Eloise, Jessica is massively swollen, her skin mottled with green and purple splotches. Her blood tests show her kidneys and heart are shutting down. Even as we try to start treatment to try and turn it around she is rapidly going the other way. I fetch my registrar, but by the time we enter there is nothing more to do, Jessica's heart has stopped for a third and final time.

I call her father, who's just got home. He knows why I'm calling, the call that no parent should ever have to receive. He is silent as I let him know what has happened and then he says just four leaden words. "I'm on my way".

With a sigh, I carry on my twilight round.

**

And then there was Sadia. Sadia was just nineteen. While working as a sailing instructor she started to have slight pains in her chest. Not worried at first she ignored it for weeks, until she found herself finding it harder and harder to catch her breath as she loaded and unloaded the training dinghies at her club up and down the foreshore. One night she found herself gasping for breath and in a panic called the ambulance. In the emergency department the doctor was puzzled; Sadia's lungs sounded normal, but her tests showed her blood oxygen was abnormally low. Thinking of a blood clot they arranged a CT scan of Sadia's lungs, which showed the problem, although not the one they were expecting. A spindly mass, larger than Sadia's head was pushing out from the middle of her thorax, compressing her lungs and arteries and heart. An urgent biopsy confirmed the devastating diagnosis: a very rare and aggressive cancer called mediastinal lymphoma.

Sadia had spent months in hospital by the time she came down to the unit. Her tumour had been irradiated, hit with traditional and experimental chemotherapy, immunotherapy, even some surgery. But it had just kept coming back. Sadia had had good days, but now her lungs were compressed to such an extent she required high pressure oxygen just to physically get air into her. This meant placing a special inflatable transparent bubble over Sadia's head, that could maintain a high pressure. We called this the "hood". It's incredibly uncomfortable, like having your head stuck in a hot wind tunnel, but it does mean you can talk out of it with some difficulty.

I entered quietly to find Sadia awake, breathing steadily, wearing the hood. Her mum was curled asleep in a chequered blanket by her bedside.

"Hi Sadia. Sorry to disturb."

Sadia nodded, and gave a weak wave, and a little smile.

"You doing okay?"

She nodded again.

I examined her and reviewed the medications and blood tests but everything was stable, nothing to change.

"Any questions for me?"

Sadia just looked at me, and then looked at her nurse, Rowena. Rowena nodded her head towards the door.

Understanding, I followed Rowena outside. She was straight to the point. It's quite common for intensive care nurses to bond closely with their patients, it's the only department in the hospital where a single nurse will look after a single patient for an entire shift.

"She wants to take the hood off"

"Okay." I pause. "Does she know what that would mean?"

Rowena nods.

"She knows. She's had enough."

I pause. I nod.

"Tell her we'll come and speak to her about it in the morning."
This isn't a decision we can make overnight. It's the hardest medical, legal and ethical discussion there is. We handover what Rowena has told me and over the next few days the consultants start the process. First they switch Sadia to high-pressure nasal oxygen so they can actually speak to her for short periods. She's clear-eyed and concise and brave and understanding. Sadia has to support her own mother through her decision, which unfortunately is often the case. The ITU team asks the symptom control specialists and her cancer team to see and together they plan how best to stop the invasive treatments.

I wasn't there at the end. Sadia took off her own oxygen, we made sure she was in no pain or distress, and surrounded by her family. A few minutes later, she died. Would that we could all show such dignity in the end.

**

The UK has a mixed history when it comes to treatment and care of cancer patients. On the one hand the National Health Service is home to some of the most cutting-edge cancer research, screening programmes and treatments in the world. The UK founded the hospice movement in 1967[61], creating hospitals and care specifically designed to treat the symptoms of suffering in those with a terminal illness.
On the other hand the UK is starting to lag behind the rest of Europe with our diagnosis and treatment of many cancers[62]. It's not entirely clear why this is, and may be a function of how we record our cancer patients compared to other countries. This however seems less likely than the obvious: for the largest four cancer types (breast, prostate, lung and colon) you are less likely to survive in the UK compared to your counterpart in Norway or Sweden. Overall cancer rates of survival in the UK are improving, but at a rate somewhat behind everybody else.
Worse still, our targets for meeting cancer waiting times and even cancer surgery times are slipping. The National Health Service has a target of sixty-two days from the GP referring for a suspected cancer to being seen by a specialist and starting the first treatment. Just under nine weeks. This target hasn't been met for years.[63] Not all cancers respond to early diagnosis and treatment, but many do.

---

61 Dame Cicely Saunders, founder of the modern hospice movement, dies. BMJ [Internet]. 2020 Feb 6 [cited 2020 Feb 13];

62 Walters S, Benitez-Majano S, Muller P, Coleman MP, Allemani C, Butler J, et al. Is England closing the international gap in cancer survival? Br J Cancer. 2015 Sep 1;113(5):848–60.

63 76% in Dec 2019 - Statistics » Provider-based Cancer Waiting Times for December 2019 (Provisional) [Internet]. [cited 2020 Feb 13]. Available from:

The drivers of this fall in cancer care are many, but chief is the failure to maintain services in the UK, particularly in cancer care, in relation to demand. We aren't doing nearly enough to keep up with our European neighbours in terms of funding, beds, nurses or doctors.

A Lancet[64] report looked at the impact of the financial crash of 2008 on global outcomes from cancer. In developed countries where unemployment was linked to health care the researchers estimated 260,000 excess deaths occurred due to cancer alone that otherwise wouldn't if the crash had not occurred.

In healthcare, money means lives, and for a decade at least we haven't invested enough. What impact this will have over the next ten years, time will tell.

**

In the past ten years, four of my close family members, one friend and one colleague were all diagnosed with a type of cancer. One didn't survive, three are in remission, two are having active treatment.

To the individual the cellular biology, the statistics, the political financial wrangling is all meaningless. A shadow is cast over the future, that came from nowhere and only offers a narrow route of escape. Grappling with that shadow can be as tough for that person's loved ones as it is for themselves, and to a lesser extent the staff looking after them. It's easy to lose hope about the world when faced with such tragic hopelessness every day. I have to remind myself that working in hospital is the thin end of the wedge of cancer care – the majority takes place in the community, with outpatient chemotherapy and scans and with generally very well patients. The hospital side is the rare and extreme end, and has probably distorted my view of oncology dramatically. Having said that my time in intensive care and then in oncology afterwards were some of the hardest months of my career. I know I couldn't do that for a lifetime, and thank God for those men and women who chose to instead.

64 Maruthappu M, Watkins J, Noor AM, Williams C, Ali R, Sullivan R, et al. Economic downturns, universal health coverage, and cancer mortality in high-income and middle-income countries, 1990-2010: a longitudinal analysis. Lancet. 2016 Aug 13;388(10045):684–95.

Coronaries

The exact moment I knew I wanted to become a cardiologist was January 18th 2013 at 11.53am. At 11.51am one of my patients, David, had a cardiac arrest.

I had admitted David into hospital the night before. David was 52 but he exuded such a bounding energy that he was often mistook for a man in his thirties. His sun-tanned youthful face was always broken into a big square smile. His age was only given away by the laughter lines that creased the corners of his bright green eyes and his head of slicked back white hair. David had been in the Royal Air Force and then ran his own business for a decade after. Still in military-fit shape, David had been surprised when he'd been told the chest pains he had been having for a week or so were likely a small heart attack.

Anxiously waiting by his side, Cat, his wife of twenty plus years, had shouted for help as David slumped over with a gasp of air as he reached for his tea. That was at 11.50am. Already hooked up to a monitor we could see the problem straight away: the electricity in David's heart had suddenly flipped from a slow and ordered heartbeat to a racing, disorganised surge of muscle twitching, beating 250 times a minute. At that speed enough blood can't physically get into the heart between beats to be effectively pumped out. No blood was getting to his brain or to his vital organs.

The crash alarm is pulled and we all run around to David's bedside. A nurse immediately starts chest compressions to try to get the heart beating properly again. It is 11.51am.

We scramble to get the defibrillator pads on quickly. We stick two large electrodes to the front of the chest and hook them up to a big battery. The monitor shows David's heart tracing in real-time: thrumming with the jagged spikes of an often deadly rhythm we call ventricular tachycardia. Meera, the senior medical doctor on the wards that morning, takes his pulse: nothing. She calls to get ready to give a shock.

The nurse keeps going with the chest compressions while Meera charges the defibrillator, then she gives the command. "Clear". It's now 11.52am.

Everyone steps back from David, Meera does a three point check to make sure no one is touching David otherwise they will be electrocuted as well when the machine goes off. Then with a shout of "shocking" Meera presses the flashing red button. The electrical pulse stimulates every muscle in David's body to contract simultaneously. David's body jerks off the bed a centimetre and then he drops back and one of the nurses tries to restart compressions as per the algorithm.

David however groans and pushes her away as he half-rolls to one side. We check his pulse and blood pressure: his heart has flipped back into a normal slow lub-dub rhythm and he has a strong pulse once more. David is trying to sit up. I'm stunned; thirty seconds ago he was essentially dying and now he is reaching for his tea. We bring Cat back, who is visibly shaken but cheered to see David as he is already trying to open his eyes. David pulls himself up to a sitting position and rubs his chest a bit. He groans and takes a deep breath, orientating himself again.

11.53am. David looks around, sees Cat and takes her hand.

"Bit sore" he says, rubbing his chest again.

I am dumbstruck. Meera comes forward.

"Sorry Mr Galaway, we had to jump on your chest and give the heart a shock to make it beat again."

David gives a nod of understanding. I forget he's been in the RAF and must've done a fair bit of first aid training himself.

"Well." He turns to his wife and gives a wry smile. "No one's ridden me like that for years!"

David is laughing, Cat is laughing, the whole cardiac arrest team is laughing, all of us nearly in hysterics to see this man go from beyond death's door to making dirty jokes in under two minutes.

It's always hard to know how to choose a specialty. How do you take the whole spectrum of medicine and surgery you train in and choose a single thing to do for the rest of your life? As a junior doctor your senior colleagues are always asking you "What do you want to do?"

Looking around at this surreal scene, this dead man so dramatically and vividly once again full of life, I make a decision. This. I'm going to do this.

**

The heart throughout ancient history was seen as the centre of human consciousness. In Ancient Greece, Plato wrote extensively about the heart; "every heart sings a song, incomplete, until another heart whispers back".[65] His protégé Aristotle went even further, claiming the heart as the "seat and source of sensation" whilst simultaneously dismissing the brain as merely "for the cooling of blood"[66]. Later Galen, considered to be the father of modern medicine, wrote a treatise on his philosophy of mind and body. He regurgitated an old idea of a "tripartite soul"[67] with the "rational soul" in the brain, the "appetitive soul" within the liver and "the spiritual soul" inside the heart.

What was it that led ancient philosophers to identify the heart as this vital organ, the "seat and source" of the human condition? The earliest writers attributed its importance to its central position, claiming it was the first structure to form in the developing foetus (still accurate) and noting anecdotally damage to the heart almost always led to death within minutes. Despite our modern day knowledge of the brain and nervous system, our increasing understanding of the neurobiology of the brain and the organic basis of our emotions, the idea that the heart still harbours a vital function of human experience, namely love, persists to this day. The modern day symbol for love remains a simple representation of the chambers of the heart. Interestingly, the idea that our anatomical heart and our "spiritual souls", our loving selves, are intertwined does indeed have some basis in modern medicine.

**

I have only ever received one written compliment in my career as a doctor. Whether that's an indictment of my practice or my patients, either or both, I'll leave it up to you to decide. It's an A5 letter, folded crisply down the centre, handwritten with the address in the top right-hand corner and signed at the bottom in a flowery hand, "Best Wishes, Ann".

---

65 Plato P. The Complete Plato by Plato. 1819 p.

66 CLARKE E, STANNARD J. Aristotle on the Anatomy of the Brain. Journal of the History of Medicine and Allied Sciences. 1963;18(2):130-48.

67 Schiefsky M. Galen and the tripartite soul. In 2012. p. 331-49.

I first met Ann on the orthopaedic ward at a large specialist hospital in the Home Counties. Ann had lived in the area all her life, and up until very recently had shared a neat cottage with her husband at the edge of town for nearly fifty years. The weeks leading up to Ann's admission to hospital had been some of the hardest of her life. Her late husband Patrick had been unwell with advanced prostate cancer for several years, needing more and more care, going through progressively punishing rounds of chemotherapy, with each one becoming ever more frail. Ann, herself in her late seventies, had been just about managing to look after the house and Patrick, and at their last cancer appointment Patrick's cancer appeared to have been responding. Hopeful for a little while, they'd even booked a holiday, their first in years, while Patrick was still well enough to travel. Then, one Tuesday morning, Ann found Patrick cold and unmoving in bed. He'd passed away suddenly overnight, possibly from a blood clot but Ann never found out. They arranged the funeral a few days later, but in her distress getting ready and trying to organise everyone Ann tripped, fell and fractured her right hip. Even for the orthopaedic specialists it was an impressively awful fracture. I still remember the air whistling through the teeth of my registrar as he looked at Ann's scans: her hip bone had sheared off and twisted in on itself. Ann, distraught while surrounded by loving family still in their funeral outfits, underwent an emergency hip replacement the following day.

I met Ann that next morning. She looked tiny and drawn, so frail despite the hulking metal prostheses I'd seen in the X-ray meeting now cemented where her hip had once been. We said our hellos, checked on her pain medication and blood tests, asked her if she had any questions. Being an ex-primary school teacher she had this wonderfully melodic voice. No matter how quietly or meekly she spoke you couldn't help but pay rapt attention.

"I do feel a bit nauseous still." She gave a weak smile, and gestured to the untouched breakfast tray next to her. "I couldn't quite manage anything except a bit of tea." We prescribed some anti-sickness medications and started to move off to the next patient.

"Any other questions?" Dr Bode, my orthogeriatric consultant asked.

Ann hesitated.

"I don't mean to be a bother" she started. "But when should I expect the pain to get better?"

Dr Bode gave me a look of consternation. We'd already asked about her hip pain and had a conversation about it. Concerned Ann was forgetful she turned back to her.

"Ann, are you still in pain from the hip?"

"No, no we discussed that already" Now it was Ann's turn to look askance at Dr Bode, as if she was the one confused. "I mean the pain here, in my chest?" Ann pointed to the left side of her torso, a handbreadth from the breastbone, just beneath her nipple. "Here, in my heart."

Concerned, we started over with Ann: re-examining her, looking at her heart electrical tracing and ordering some more blood tests. A few hours later the laboratory was so worried about the test results they phoned me directly.

"Hello. Are you a member of Dr Bode's team?"

"Uh. Yes" Still very junior as this was only my second year as a doctor. "I'm the house officer."

"We have Ann O'Reilly's troponin result to give." My heart beat a little faster. The lab only phoned through results that are wildly abnormal or dangerous, otherwise they just pop up onto our computer screen when they are ready. Troponin is the blood marker for heart damage.

"Go ahead" I said, pen and paper poised.

"It's 10,320."

"Okay..." New to the hospital and not anywhere near a computer I asked. "And what is the normal value here?"

"Less than 4."

"Oh. Thank you."

**

Ann would end up staying in the hospital for nearly four weeks. Firstly, her hip operation and the recovery time was complicated by the concern she was now having a massive heart attack, the treatment for which is blood thinning medication, which, in someone who's just had their leg sliced open, their bone sawn through and rebuilt out of metal can lead to a much higher risk of further bleeding. Cardiologists started appearing on the ward to look at Ann. They would pass off jobs to me as I hovered in the background; repeat her blood tests and ECGs, ask the orthopaedic team about the blood thinning medications, request an ultrasound scan of her heart. Ann was obviously very worried.

"Am I going to die?" she asked me, between visitations from bone doctors and elderly care doctors and heart doctors.

"Everyone's doing the best they can, and you're doing really well Ann." I told her. She was grateful, but I hadn't really answered her question. To be honest I really didn't know the answer.

The cardiologists took Ann down a few days later for another procedure, this time to look inside the coronary arteries, the three vital blood vessels that supply the tissue of the heart itself, to find the blockage that had caused Ann's heart attack and try to open it up again. Except when they went inside the heart, they found no problem at all. Ann hadn't had a heart attack. We were all baffled.

"What does this mean?" she asked me, as confused as I was.

"I don't know. But I'll try and find someone who might." And I dashed off to find a cardiologist to come and speak to Ann.

It was only when the scan of her heart happened that the diagnosis changed. I remember standing at the bedside as the sonographer brought up a blue-white and black picture of Ann's beating heart, all four chambers moving in real time. Catching my obviously oblivious expression the sonographer pointed the anatomy out to Ann and myself.

"These are the top chambers of the heart, the atrium, and here are the bottom chambers, the ventricles." The sonographer traced the outline of the left ventricle, the main pumping muscle for the body. At its base it flared out into a bubble of flesh that was hardly moving. The sonographer tapped at it on the screen. "There, there is the problem."

Ann looked at me questioningly again, and again, I went to find someone who could answer.

**

Flash forward five years and that's now my job. Ann was suffering from an actual cardiac condition called Broken Heart Syndrome.

Described in Japan only relatively recently in 1991 the proper term for the condition is Takotsubo's Cardiomyopathy[68]. The word "Takotsubo" literally means "octopus pot", derived from the appearance of the heart that the sonographer was so concerned about. The rounding of the tip of the left ventricle resembles the specifically shaped fishing pots used to catch octopus in Japan.

Broken Heart syndrome typically occurs after a major life event or trauma, or in Ann's case, both. We don't understand the exact mechanics of it but we believe the surge in stress hormones created by a highly intense emotional state creates an unbearable strain on the heart muscle in certain individuals. Clinically this can look like anything from a fleeting chest pain to a heart attack to complete heart failure and occasionally, death. These patients literally die from a broken heart.

**

---

[68] Sealove BA, Tiyyagura S, Fuster V. Takotsubo cardiomyopathy. J Gen Intern Med. 2008 Nov;23(11):1904–8.

Fortunately for Ann, deadly as Takotsubo's can be, it's also generally reversible. As the mind recovers, so does the heart. For Ann that meant grieving, and having missed Patrick's funeral that was hard indeed. Ann occupied the corner bed by the window in the unit for nearly a month all in, as her rehab progressed slowly. I took a few students to examine her heart and look at her pictures. I felt my own awe echoed back to me afresh each time we visited with new medical students, as they tried to wrap their head around this concept of literally worrying yourself to death. Ann recovered well, and eventually a month later she was ready to go home. She told me she was still going on that holiday.

"Patrick would've gone spare if I'd wasted the money." She confided in me, with a light chuckle, and off she went.

A few days later a letter arrived on the ward addressed to me. A few kind words and a thank you. I've never been so touched. It's easy to forget what an impact the smallest gestures can have. There are some patients that you never forget, their histories become built into the fabric and foundation of who you are as a professional. Ann was one of those patients.

**

Conditions like Takotsubo's demonstrate that perhaps the Greek fathers of medicine weren't far off when they wondered if the physical heart and our spiritual existence are intertwined. More than any other organ we still associate the heart with our emotional inner lives. Empathy "pulls on the heartstrings", anxiety "sets the heart aflutter", we can "have a change of heart" or wear "our hearts on our sleeves". Our hearts can be heavy, or cold, or indeed broken. They can even belong to someone else.

**

There's an evocative episode of the BBC Television series Doctor Who written by the fiction author Neil Gaiman entitled "The Doctor's Wife"[69]. Rather than referencing a love interest the titular character is actually the Doctor's TARDIS, her work. That embodiment of one's work as a spouse is particularly apt in medicine. It's a career you choose young, that most will stay committed to for lifelong, and never really leaves you, even when you're away. A vocation such as medicine often feels like a second marriage. Ironically many doctors will end up also marrying another doctor or other health professional, for a variety of reasons.

---

[69] BBC One - Doctor Who, Series 6, The Doctor's Wife [Internet]. BBC. [cited 2020 Feb 13].

1. You spend most of your twenties in University with other medical students or in hospitals with other health professionals

2. The job puts an enormous pressure on your social and love lives. Not only a strain on your time but also an emotional toll it can be hard for a non-medic to understand.

**

It's the middle of January in 2007, I'm standing outside Euston station in a suit of golden Roman centurion armour. At least that's the idea: I'm actually wearing scraps of spray-painted cardboard held together with scotch tape. Underneath I'm just in my boxers. It's about five degrees Celsius. The outfit is so flimsy one of my flatmates is running behind me, scooping up sections that fell off and hastily taping them back on like a boxer's cut man.

If I'd known at the time I'm about to meet my future wife I'd have probably rethought my outfit, but as it is I'm concentrating on the street fundraising event I'm supposed to be running and keeping my armour from disintegrating, leaving me naked holding a bucket outside Euston station on an icy Saturday morning.

So when I see Dilsan for the first time I'm somewhat off my game. She's dressed up like all of us medical students, although she's chosen a more sensible outfit; winter clothes plus a pink tutu, pink wand and sparkly bubble-gum pink wings.

From the moment I see her suddenly all those clichés make sense: I can physically feel a slight pull in my chest towards her. When we share a brief moment of conversation my heart pounds. A few days later we bump into each other in the union, and from that moment forward I feel a golden line extending from my heart into the future. Our future.

**

Flash forward seven years and I'm standing in my wedding suit, foot tapping on the orchard floor, waiting to see Dilsan appear at the tree line. This is our wedding day in my parent's garden, a beautiful blistering day in July. A hundred of our family and closest friends sit patiently waiting. The music starts, and I catch a glimpse of white dress in dappled sunlight through a break in the trees. She's the most beautiful thing I've ever seen. My heart is in my throat. I can feel myself tearing up.

**

In being married to a doctor there are upsides and downsides. On the one hand, we are both inside the tent of the medical menagerie, can readily understand the other's trials and help solve their problems. My wife gives me surgical advice and I give her medical advice.

On the other hand, we can too often carry our work home with us and the demands of the on-call shifts stack together, triply so with two children. This is a particular concern for junior doctors, trying to juggle childcare, training, on-calls and all the other modern requisites of a medical career: audit, teaching, courses. This was hard enough when my time was my own, now my time is also my kid's time; the minutes I spend at home working on something are minutes I don't give them. The struggle to be a Good Doctor and a Good Parent is something I think all generations of emergency professionals have had to deal with. Trying to get childcare at six am, or at five pm when the on-call relief has called in sick, while the crash bleep goes off and the patients pile up, is probably the most stressful experience I've ever had. The hospitals I've worked in have sometimes been supportive, sometimes quite the opposite. A high number of doctors leave medicine each year, many citing such pressures as the reason. We need to take as good care of those looking after the patients as we do the patients themselves.

**

Cardiology for me is all the best bits of being a doctor. The heart may not be the "seat and source" of the human soul, but it sits at the centre of modern medicine, alone or alongside many other illnesses; whether that's a primary heart problem or a brain problem or a kidney problem. It's challenging to manage that complexity and rewarding. "Doing things" is relatively rare in modern medicine: we are more cautious, more conservative, and more considered with all our interventions. Cardiology is an exception: we do things all the time, shock patients, thread wires into heart vessels, valves and electrical pathways, implant pacemakers, scan patients in six different ways. And, unusual again in modern medicine, you get a tangible result. David's miraculous recovery was rare, but by far the most satisfying as a doctor I've experienced. It's an illusion to think we can "fix people", but nowhere comes closer in medicine (excluding surgery) than cardiology. That's why I love the heart. Maybe you will too.

Meiosis

It's January 2016. I've just finished a set of four nights, and I rush home to enjoy a rare shared day off with Dilsan. She meets me at the door, holding a white stick with a blue symbol on it.

"Are you ready to be a Daddy?"

My sleep-deprived brain can't process what she means. What is she holding? A Daddy? Right now? I feel sweaty. I need to sit down. Some distant fuzzy part of my brain is shouting but I can't hear it.

Dilsan's bright smile is fading into a concerned frown.

"Dom are you okay?"

The brain knocks again and this time gets through. That's a pregnancy test, this is your wife, she's telling you something.

"We're having a baby?" I know I'm not giving the reaction I'm supposed to but all the cogs are frozen and the machine is out for repairs.

Dilsan gives my hand a squeeze.

"We are having a baby."

**

The cells that make up the two halves of the spark of life, the ovum and the sperm, form themselves through a unique process called meiosis.

Meiosis is the process by which cells divide their DNA into half the normal amount ready to combine with another to make a new human being. Confused? Imagine all of the DNA in your body as a set of encyclopaedias, each "book" in the set is a sticky string of bunched up genes called a "chromosome", and there are 23 books to make up the whole set. Each book is full of instructions to tell your cells what to do. Every cell in the body has two entire sets of encyclopaedias, one inherited from your mother and one inherited from your father.

When your cells, specifically the sperm and ova, go through meiosis they have to divide up their encyclopaedias to hold only one set of chromosomes, so they are ready to combine with their opposite number to form a new set of two again in a new combination; a new child. If this doesn't happen, and more than two sets of genes make it into a cell, the instructions they give become confused and can cause problems with the normal function of the child. This is what happens in Down syndrome for example.

This process of dividing two sets of genes into one is random, which "book" from which set of genes makes it into the final sperm or egg is chance. You could have 23 books from your mother, or 23 from your father, or any combination in between. Then there is a process of swapping portions of the chromosomes as well, again random. This would be like you dividing the sets of encyclopaedias and then randomly ripping out pages from each book and swapping them with their counterpart pages in the other set. All of this random combination is the basis of mutation, and mutation is the basis for evolution.

How those genes then come out in the child, how they are expressed, depends on what they are combined with and which genes are expressed preferentially over the others. This is how the variety of all living things is generated. Your brothers and sisters from the same parents are essentially just different rolls of the same dice that made you.

For men meiosis occurs constantly, but for women it occurs only once. Before a woman is even born, when she herself is still in her mother's womb, she forms the ovum that will lie in her ovaries and one day make her own children. When a woman carries a baby girl she is essentially carrying her own grandchildren as well. My wife pointed this out to me when we were told a few months later we were having a daughter, a chain of our own children and grandchildren stretching into the future. Human reproduction is the most astounding of miracles but from the very start of my career I've seen first-hand that it can also be the most difficult of maladies.

**

It's 2011, I am still a medical student a year from qualification and I am sitting sweating in the only air conditioned ward in the hospital. This is the Intensive Care unit in Tupua Tamasese Meaole Hospital, the largest hospital in Samoa. Outside the doors several large dogs lie panting in the tropical heat.

The ward only has one occupant at the moment. Teuila (*tay-wee-lah*) is in her mid-twenties, fourteen weeks pregnant, and dying of something no one understands.

I have been in Samoa for nearly five weeks by now. It's a curious mix of Western modern culture and ancient Pacific tradition. In the city there are colossal problems with many of the same chronic illnesses the industrialised world is dealing with: diabetes, obesity, kidney damage. The McDonald's "Teen" meal here is a double cheeseburger, fries, milkshake and chicken nuggets. The "Teen" meal is actually two meals. Like a cultural disease the city families are late catching on to the same dangerous health fads affecting the rest of the modern world. When we go out on the vaccine bus, the city folk are more likely to refuse vaccinating their children because of fears over the MMR that they've read on the Internet. This is in a country where most of these diseases are still in living memory, if not still active.[70]

Out in the rural areas it's a completely different world. Extended families still live together in clusters of small wooden houses centred around a single open air structure, the "fale tele" or family meeting place. Mostly farmers and workers, occasionally commuting to the city to work as cleaners or nannies, the poverty here is startling compared to their city counterparts. Interestingly they willingly accept vaccinations when we visit on the vaccine bus, the women pulling all the available children to the centre "fale tele". Despite this acceptance of modern medicine in the rural communities, there is also a problem with traditional herbal healers, the Taulasea, delaying very sick patients coming to hospital. Sometimes too late to be able to help them.

Teuila was one of these patients. When she was brought into hospital all of her uncovered skin was caked in a muddy-brown paste, wrapped in leaves and herbs. She was emaciated, delirious, staring wild-eyed all about her. From the limited story I could gather from our teaching rounds she had become pregnant a few months before, and developed morning sickness very soon after. Her vomiting had been incessant for weeks. Rather than come to hospital she'd been visited by a Taulasea who had applied herbal medicines, pastes and blessings, and continued to do so for weeks more. By the time she'd come to hospital her body was in freefall; she'd no doubt lost the baby, her kidneys and liver were shutting down, her heart was starting to show signs of failure, she'd lost all coherent speech and, even after days of tests and rehydration and treatment, she wasn't getting any better. Her abdomen was swollen, at first I assumed from her pregnancy, but later recognised the full body wasting and abdominal swelling of extreme nutrition deficiency.

---

[70] Indeed, about eight years after we were there, Samoa had one of the largest outbreaks of measles in its history, with nearly a hundred children dying.

At the time, all the advanced maternal medicine I had rattling in my head had been gleaned from episodes of "House". I spent a lot of days sitting in that ICU, flipping through her blood tests and then my textbooks, trying to figure out what was wrong with her. I never did. No one did.

The closest I came was wondering if she had a very rare condition sometimes seen in pregnancy associated with intractable vomiting called Wet Beri Beri[71]. *bæri bæri* is Sinhalese for "I cannot, I cannot" and was originally described in Indonesia in the 1500s. Essentially the body loses so much of a vitamin called thiamine that every organ, especially heart and brain, starts to fail.

We left the country a week later. I still don't know what was wrong with Teuila. It's easy to forget in modern industrialised countries like ours just how dangerous and mysterious pregnancy can really be.

**

Eight years later and I find myself thinking the exact same thing.

I'm sitting in the Cardiology offices watching the autumn foliage sway gently in the bright October sun. I've been a cardiology registrar for just six weeks. My bleep goes off and my heart sinks when I see the extension. Maternity.

I cautiously picked up the phone.

"Hello Cardiology?"

"Hi, this is the obstetric registrar, we need you down here immediately."

"I'm on my way."

As I bowl out of the ward and into the breezy sunshine I don't stop to reflect on why obstetrics is the one department I don't ask any questions of. Maternal medicine, the science of looking after both mother and child as both undergo astoundingly complex biological changes, is something that has frightened me since those days in Samoa. My stomach-churning experience with Fatma and the river of blood probably hasn't helped and since having children myself everything baby-related sends me into a twitchy anxiety.

I duck into the maternity wing, flash the security guards my ID despite my scrubs and stethoscope and they open the doors for me. The maternity registrar is waiting. Marcella is five-two, mid-forties, Italian, strict blonde hair tied back in a single ponytail. She's direct, dedicated, unflappable. Not overly nice though.

"Hurry up. She's just through here."

Marcella leads me through the Labour ward, the occasional scream escapes from the delivery suites as we pass. She tells me about the case as we walk.

---

[71] Chisolm-Straker M, Cherkas D. Altered and unstable: wet beriberi, a clinical review. J Emerg Med. 2013 Sep;45(3):341-4.

Grace is 26, in her first pregnancy and had up to that point had no problems at all with her or the baby. She came in today when she felt a painful hardening in her stomach, coming back and forth at regular intervals. At thirty-eight weeks she knew the drill. These were contractions; her baby was ready to come into the world. She'd come into the department and been wheeled into triage and then panicked as the nurse doing her observations checked them over and over again nervously, before calling Marcella who had called me. The baby was fine, but it was Grace's heart rate that had the problem; it had dropped abnormally low. Marcella thrust an ECG in front of me before we reached her room. I glanced at it; complete heart block, a dangerous heart rhythm.

"She needs a pacemaker. Right away" I said, out loud, slightly confused a young lady would ever develop this problem, although it sometimes occurs in pregnancy. A pacemaker is a box with wires that can keep the heart beating when it slows down, although we rarely put them in in anyone under fifty. I'm way outside my comfort zone. Marcella gave me a deadpan look as we entered the birthing suite.

"Tell that to the baby."

I followed Marcella in to find Grace swearing and panting as she had another contraction. Grace was already in labour. Her heart rate sits at 40, low enough to make a normal person pass out, and yet she is doing the biological equivalent of sprinting. I do what any trainee doctor in my position should do when faced with a tricky mother-baby situation: I call the boss. My consultant that day also happens to be the departmental lead. He listens carefully to the story without interrupting, then pauses. "I'll be right down".

A few minutes later my boss Dr Raj is peering at the ECGs next to me. He crosses his arms and looks pensively back and forth, between Grace, still huffing away in contractions, her heart monitor, and back to the ECG again. "So what shall we do?" I ask, so relieved by Dr Raj's mere presence I almost sound casual.

He pauses to give the whole scene another calculating look.

"Nothing."

I'm stunned, but just an hour later Dr Raj is proved 100% right. Grace gives birth to a healthy 8lb baby girl who she names Ayla. Which is a name very close to my heart.

**

When pregnancy goes wrong it can be terrifying. When it goes right it is simply overwhelming. It's 2011, I am a student back on an obstetric rotation, and I am scrubbed and gowned at the back of an operating theatre on labour ward, trying to peer over the shoulder of the doctors. The dome of surgical lights flooding the surgical field is a white so bright it's nearly blue. Between the periwinkle surgical gowns, I catch glimpses of pale mocha flesh and a sudden scarlet flash as they make the opening incision into the abdomen. This is the first time I'd ever attended a birth. I can't remember the name of the couple, but I remember they were both South Asian young professionals and both jumpy in a happy but anxious way. There's more pushing and pulling, I can make out the daffodil yellow of internal abdominal fat followed by flashes of rose-red blood and then the deep pink of the muscular womb itself. Another slash and a slosh of fluid as the waters break, and then emerges a crying purple-pink perfect baby girl. The paediatrician bundles her onto the resuscitaire and I follow, slightly overwhelmed by what I'm witnessing. I'm surprised to find the theatre air conditioning so cold on my cheeks. I touch them, they are wet with tears. I can't really explain what I expected but I didn't expect such an emotional response to a stranger's child. The first time you witness a birth I challenge you to not react the same way. Most of us cried that first time. Those who'll admit to it at least. Once the new-born is all wrapped up the midwife wants to pass her to her dad.

"Hold on" he says "We want to do skin to skin." He steps back and starts to undress. Bemused, the midwife hands this precious bundle to me. "Here, hold her for a second"

I'm staring down at this tiny face, looking up at me.

"Welcome to the world" I say.

I pass her across to her father and return back to where I'm supposed to be, observing the operation.

**

The next time I'm standing in that room, it's September 2016, the Mum on the operating table is my wife, Dilsan. We've had a mostly alright pregnancy, one or two minor scares, but for the most part we've been lucky. We both trained in this hospital, and one or two of the team that day we happen to have been students under all those years ago. It's comfortingly familiar.

They put the drape up and I am suddenly on the patient side, me and Dilsan both.

I want to hold her hand but I can't, so I just stroke her head. I keep stealing glances at her observations every ten seconds on the monitor visible to my left. I can't switch the inner doctor off, even though I wish I could.

It seems like just a minute swooshes by and then they are raising our daughter above the drape, her pudgy purple face still a little bloody, screwed up in an angry cry. It's the first time I ever see her face but it's like I've known it for years. I feel like I recognise her, that this was how it was always going to be. I'm much more composed than I thought I would be. I follow her across to the resuscitaire, the same station as before, but now the child's my own. They offer me to cut the cord and I find I don't want to. I'm happy to just stare at her. And then I'm holding her, bringing her back to Dilsan to see for the first time herself. This is our daughter. We name her Ayla.

**

It was never certain we would have children, for a variety of reasons. Even when I found out Dilsan was pregnant it was really hard as the father to make it seem real. For doctors, we were surprisingly superstitious about it, more than a little bit fed by our own experiences looking after sick children and mothers. Dilsan being a surgeon had this even worse than I did. We wouldn't even tell anyone the name we had chosen. We barely spoke it to each other; we used a code name, "Moon Baby", after the meaning of the word Ayla: "the glow of light around the moon".

No one tells you quite a few things about being a parent. Firstly, babies are so noisy. Ayla's snorts and grunts while she slept kept me in a state of nervous tension for her first few weeks. She was so loud she sounded like she was searching for truffles. Funnily enough when we moved her into her own room six months later the silence disturbed me even more.

Secondly, your own children are hilarious. They make you laugh in a way it's impossible to describe in words. Becoming a father had a profound impact on every aspect of my life. I decided to reset all my priorities, my family came first. I went back to work, quit my blog and decided to work to live, not the other way around. I cut out all the unhealthy snacks and sugary treats. I now needed to be there for my children and my grandchildren.

I became a huge feminist. Not that I was particularly unsupportive of women's rights before my daughter was born, quite the opposite. But now I found myself swearing loudly in children's baby aisles when I found only pink princess clothes, shouting at the radio when some moron made a sexist or ignorant comment. I want my daughter to feel there is nothing she cannot achieve in life. Not so long ago the three most powerful people in the country were women; the Prime Minister, the Queen, the President of the Supreme Court. Not to mention the Met Police Commissioner, the Fire Commissioner and the Presidents of the Royal Colleges of Medicine and Surgery, and most importantly of all, Doctor Who.

I want her to believe she can do anything. Personally I think all parents live a little vicariously through their children, so I'd like her to be an astronaut. I have great concerns about how we will get her there. Both of us being doctors, with gruelling night shifts, weekends and long days, childcare is an incredible hurdle for us. We may end up quitting, or going part time or out of training if it compromises our ability to be there for them.

I'm often asked how having young children affects my work. I have to say generally I think it has made me better. For one thing, I'm usually too tired to get excited or anxious about anything, a dispassionate objectivity that has eluded me for most of my career. Also being in the system as a patient made me realise how valuable and precious the NHS is, how truly life changing it can be when things go right, and when things go wrong. I also balance life and work in a much healthier way. I make sure I spend my odd days with my family, and we make the most of them.

There are some downsides. Difficult nights turn into stressful days. I can't seem to ignore the babies crying in A&E anymore. The odd missed baby-food stain on a work jumper that I scramble to cover.

I count my blessings every day however, in the first-hand knowledge that so many are not so fortunate.

Coffee

It's a sweltering day in early September 2012 and I have been a doctor for just over a month. 5pm has already come and gone, any hopes of finishing on time dashed by an emergency: a cardiac arrest. One of the surgical patients, a morbidly obese man in his late fifties looks to have had a massive heart attack and despite the best efforts of the team, he unfortunately died.

I tap the code wearily into the surgical office to find one of my fellow new doctors still here, buried under mountains of paperwork and patient lists.

I can just about make out Ayesha's tied back black hair peeking above the high backed chair she's working in, paper shuttling across the desk before her. Ayesha is the daughter of Afghani immigrants, the first doctor in her family. Trained at one of the best medical schools in the country she chose to come back to her local hospital, one of the worst in the country. Where many of us had those first day jitters, still finding our feet, Ayesha came onto the ward working like she'd been a doctor for years, not minutes.

"Still here?" She asks, without turning around.

I slump heavily into an office chair.

"Arrest." My voice is leaden. Ayesha can tell this means, as most cardiac arrests, the patient didn't survive.

"Oh. What happened??"

"Mr Jeffers, bed 8. He died"

Ayesha doesn't say anything. The papers before her lie motionless. There is silence. In my head I realise Mr Jeffers was one of Ayesha's patients. This is not how I should've told her. Idiot.

"Ayesha, are you okay?"

Ayesha turns in her chair. She is crying, very quietly.

I don't know what to do.

"Coffee?"

**

Coffee was a ritualised component of the Ancient world. The first recorded coffee drinking dates back to Yemen in the Middle Ages where Sufi monks would imbibe coffee to better hear the word of God[72]. Early coffee houses in Egypt and Iraq were a halfway house between a tea room and a temple.

The active ingredient in coffee, caffeine, is a stimulant and technically a psychoactive drug, the world's most utilised. Caffeine has effects on the heart, kidneys and muscle, but predominantly works in the brain to prevent the onset of fatigue. Over a lifetime caffeine has some deleterious effects but also many positives. In my field, the heart specifically, numerous large studies have shown strong reductions in the risk of heart disease and stroke in coffee drinkers compared to non-coffee drinkers[73]. It would seem the rituals of the ancient coffee imbibers had benefits far beyond what they imagined.

Modern medical practice is a much more recent invention but not without its own rituals, of which coffee remains an essential part.

**

Ayesha and I sat down with a coffee the next day.

"I've never had a patient die before. " she said, visibly shaken. At that point I hadn't experienced it either. It's a wave of emotion, when a patient dies unexpectedly. At first; panic. Your mind combs over every detail of the case, looking for something you may have missed, something that may have changed the outcome. Sometimes guilt. Did I push hard enough for that scan to be done? Did I try this treatment plan for long enough? After guilt comes sadness, especially when that loss is made more real by witnessing the grief of the family. The hardest part comes when we realise we have to now put away those feelings entirely, because the next patient is in front of you, and needs you to be completely present. But sometimes it lingers. We are always racked with the thought there could've been something more to be done.

I don't have much to say to Ayesha, I'm even less experienced at any of this than she is. We sip our coffees, make small talk about other things, and yet, we both end up feeling a little bit better for it. Losing a patient in any circumstance is a hard feeling to live with. It's doubly hard to deal with alone.

**

---

[72] Milos G. Coffee's Mysterious Origins [Internet]. The Atlantic. 2010 [cited 2020 Feb 13].

[73] Ding Ming, Bhupathiraju Shilpa N., Satija Ambika, van Dam Rob M., Hu Frank B. Long-Term Coffee Consumption and Risk of Cardiovascular Disease. Circulation. 2014 Feb 11;129(6):643–59.

During a brief stint in neurosurgery our consultant, a very well-respected brain surgeon, would stop the ward round at 10am on the dot every single day, and march the team to the Hospital Friends canteen, where he'd order a round of coffee and Belgian buns for each of us. Whether we wanted a bun or not he would plonk it in front of us.[74] He would always pay.

"When the team goes for coffee, the boss pays." He would say.

"Why?" I asked, through a face full of Belgian bun.

"It's the rules!" He proclaimed. And that was that.

To this day I still buy all my juniors coffee if we all go together. It is, after all, "the rules". I also probably have a small fortune in Belgian bun credit to repay. The "rules" may seem antiquated, slightly silly possibly, harking from a time when medicine was long white coats and stuffy old men, but on reflection those coffee mornings were vital. Neurosurgery was an intense job: it was normal to work twelve hour days as a standard, despite also being completely illegal at the time. We often lost patients, or dealt with life-changing and horrendous complications. Infected brains, tumours that took a young woman's sight and later mobility, children with vascular deformities meaning they'd never live past five years old. Those coffee rounds were an unofficial outlet: a way to let off some pressure with the boss without the formality or stress of an official sit down. I'd listen to the training registrars complain about difficult cases, or the consultant tell them about terrible mistakes he had made, and how they could avoid them.

Coffee meant more than a quick break. This was group therapy, teaching, case review, team building and counselling all rolled into one. "The rules" were important, vital to coping with the rigours of the job.

**

You hear this phrase a lot; being a doctor is "just a job", but oddly in widely different contexts. On the one hand, the "higher calling" of medicine is derided by some, who insist it's "just a job" like any other. On the other hand, doctors under extreme pressure need to know sometimes that their work is "just a job". It should stay compartmentalised and allow them a life outside the hospital or surgery, to balance their own mental health against their working lives.

---

[74] (There's a bakery in the Covered Market in Oxford that produces the best Belgian buns I've ever had by the way. One of the few advantages to rotating around the country; you develop a random geographic knowledge of great eateries).

Which is it? I don't think anyone working in any emergency setting with human beings would accept the derogatory label of "just a job", whether that job is doctor, nurse, physiotherapist, pharmacist, fireman, policeman, or paramedic. The normal course of a human life is long periods of normality and stability, punctuated by "Life" with a capital L; births, deaths, marriages, divorces, comedy and tragedy. There's only so much of that a human mind can take, few of us can withstand constant turmoil and upheaval. That's why the mental health of those in extreme situations suffers: refugees, long-term domestic abuse and homelessness amongst others.

Being in an emergency job such as medicine means you are party to a constant stream of Life events: births, deaths, monumental illnesses. All the things that intrude into our bubble of stability to rudely remind us of what we already know but wilfully forget: life is random and hard and cruel, and important, and wonderful. So medicine isn't "just a job" in that sense. It's an enormous privilege to bear witness and to help human beings through the hardest and most real times in their lives.

However, if you let that tragedy in too much, you expose too much of yourself to that constant stream of suffering and you run the risk to your own mental health, exceeding your mind's capacity to process capital L Life events. That's why it's important to know there are others who can share your mental load, and share the physical work as well. That's exactly why we work in multidisciplinary teams. Increasingly, that team is under threat.

**

Once upon a time doctors worked in set teams called "firms". A consultant, a registrar (a senior trainee), some senior house officers (middle-grade doctors) and some brand new doctors too. Usually based on a single ward, you were embedded like a soldier in a unit, or a single part in a great engine. Over time, with the re-organisation of doctors into shift patterns this structure broke down. How can you sit down for that vitally important coffee as a team when doctor A is on nights, doctor B is on evenings, doctor C is on earlies and doctor D is on leave?

It can be incredibly isolating in the modern NHS. It's rare you will work side-by-side with anyone regularly, and of those that you do it's rarer still you will have the time or opportunity to make connections or team-build. Medical students move departments every four to six weeks. Junior doctors will change jobs every four months and change hospitals every year, for much of the first four to ten years of training. I moved house ten times in my first ten years as a medical student and junior doctor. I kept my moving boxes, once or twice I never even fully unpacked.

The first year on the battlefield was a watershed, transitioning from student to doctor. The weight of responsibility and the sheer terror forged a bond with the doctors like Ayesha I started with that stuck for life. That transformative year is truly special, but then you move on. It becomes harder and harder to make and maintain those connections with your colleagues. Life accelerates and there seems to be less and less time for "coffee".

**

That's not to say working with other doctors and team members is always easy; people are just people, and a resource-strapped high intensity environment doesn't always bring out the best in any of us. Some of the biggest mistakes I've made in my career have had nothing to do with dealing with patients but dealing with colleagues.

I'm leaving for work in the dark on an icy cold day in November. I've been a doctor for five years. My daughter is just eight weeks old and not sleeping. Nobody is sleeping. After a particularly rough day shift we've had a particularly rough night and it feels like the sun has disappeared, figuratively and literally. I remember when I started working telling my brother, who has three children, how tiring I was finding it.
"Tired?" He laughed. "You don't know what tiredness is. Wait till you have kids."
I know now what tired is. I'm up to four coffees a day at this point. I reach the station two minutes too late and watch my train slide away from the platform. I grab a coffee and deliberately sit on the arctic platform, hunched in my coat, stewing in self-pity. I catch the next train to the station then half-jog up the hill to the hospital, my breath blooming ahead of me in the cold air. I whip onto the cardiac unit ten minutes late, throw down my stuff and then join the team at the bedside for the ward round.
It's led by a senior doctor I don't know very well, Dr Spitzer. I apologise for being late, and as Dr Spitzer looks up I realise I'm still holding my coffee cup. Shit. This looks bad.
"If you'd like to finish up your coffee at the nurse's station, you can join us after."
He's smiling, but his tone is sub-zero. I'm flushing. I bin my coffee and come straight back. The ward round drags on. Dr Spitzer is short with everyone, not just me, including one or two patients. He decides a patient needs a special test at the cardiac hospital.
"Which consultant shall I refer to?" I ask, knowing the system setup is to only accept requests by one of two consultants who work at both sites.
"That question is insulting to me. I am the consultant here."

I'm not really sure what to say to that. We have got off on the wrong foot and things have soured from there. There's an awkward pause in the middle of which a crash alarm goes off.

We run round to a patient I know well, Lloyd, slumped in bed.

Lloyd is a lesson in how cruel life can be. At sixty-two he had had a routine dental hygiene appointment. Three weeks later he began to feel tired, febrile, sweating all night and exhausted all day. His GP heard a heart murmur, but didn't think much of it. Two more weeks passed, and by this time Lloyd was very sick indeed. He collapsed into our ED, profoundly septic. A full screen for infection found a strange bug in his blood, and a scan of his heart showed a clump of bacteria the size of a walnut sitting on one of his heart valves.

I looked after him on that first admission and had an incredibly fractious day trying to get him transferred for an emergency heart surgery. After much bartering and discussion, he went late one Thursday evening and was operated on a Friday morning.

He survived the surgery, but when he woke up he found he was struggling to move his left arm or leg. He'd had a stroke, an uncommon but tragic complication of his condition and the operation. Lloyd got through the recovery and started doing rehabilitation. They called a few weeks after his operation to send him back to us, his local hospital. I asked over the phone the usual questions; how were his blood tests? How were his oxygen levels? A slightly inexperienced junior doctor reeled off the latest numbers without thinking about them, his oxygen levels were far too low.

"Are you sure about that?" I asked.

"Uhhh... I'll call you back." The line went dead.

I pulled up our linked systems to look at Lloyd's X-rays. His lungs were filled with fluid. Lloyd's heart infection had come back, and eaten through his new heart valve. Lloyd went back for a second surgery the next day, and spent another week in Intensive Care. Again he started to recover, eventually making it back to us a month later. He had some trouble still with finding some words, but he had seemed in good spirits. That was yesterday.

Today we find Lloyd unresponsive, barely breathing. The team fell about him trying to resuscitate. Normally someone takes charge, leading the team to make sure timing is kept and it's organised and each moving part doesn't clash with another. Dr Spitzer is standing at the bedside; the team is looking at him. In my sleep deprived mind, I'm not sure how many seconds pass, but I'm screamingly conscious each one is time Lloyd doesn't have. Behind my eyes those seconds stretch out to minutes. Some of the juniors take the initiative and are getting drugs ready. An anaesthetist seemingly materialises from nowhere and passes a tube into Lloyd's throat. Still no one is leading. We share a look.

"Dr Spitzer are you okay to lead?" I prompt him, probably less politely than I'm writing this now. Perspective is a funny thing.

He bridles. "Yes, yes, I will lead" he shuffles around, but nothing happens. The time comes up to two minutes. I watch two separate doctors try to draw up the same drug and give it, I stop one of them. Dr Spitzer is a statue. This is getting dangerous, so I make a decision and break hierarchy. "I am leading this arrest. Is that okay Dr Spitzer?" I can't genuinely remember what he says in reply but I set about organising the team: making sure the nurse doing compressions isn't tiring, delegating a doctor to take an oxygen blood test, arranging fluid and heart pumping medications, organising a scribe and somebody to time. The team settles into the rhythm of resuscitating. We run through all the possible causes of Lloyd's deterioration. Minutes pass. The heart tracing shows a flicker of life, and then the heart springs back to beating again on its own.

I breathe a sigh of relief, but it's short-lived. He's not making any effort to breathe and his pupils aren't reacting to light. I'm not sure where Dr Spitzer has gone, but the anaesthetist wants to take Lloyd for a head scan and I go with them. The scan shows the stroke Lloyd had has got larger and there is new bleeding into it. This is a fatal complication. We speak to the brain surgeons, but they tell us what we already know; there is nothing more to be done. Lloyd passes away peacefully a few hours later.

**

Later we attempt to discuss the events of the morning. I'm shattered and frustrated and reeling from the death of a patient I knew really well. The team wants to know if anything could have gone better. A junior doctor suggests the lack of a leader to start with could have been addressed sooner. I physically feel Dr Spitzer seething next to me. I don't say a word. The resuscitation was successful, the end result was the same, nothing would've changed. Then one of the senior nurses decides to say she found me too loud during the arrest. I can't hold my tongue. I know I should stay quiet but I just snap.

"I apologise if I seemed too 'loud'. " My tone is terse. I imagine a vein pops in my head. "But there was no clear leader and it was getting dangerous".

Then Dr Spitzer erupts. I can't remember what he said or what I said in response. It's all gone wrong and a bit unprofessional. There's still quite a bit of work to do so I just leave.

**

At the end of the day Dr Spitzer calls me into his office. Tempers have flared and cooled. We sit. Things start reasonably well.

"I don't know you Dominic. Tell me about yourself."

"Well I've been a doctor for five years, and started here in November."
He leans forward.
"Yes I noticed that you have disrespected me since day one."
My eyebrows shoot into my head. What? I genuinely can't remember meeting Dr Spitzer more than twice before this week. Was he really so offended? I cross my arms, more taken aback than anything. For some reason Dr Spitzer finds this another gross misdemeanour.
"Uncross your arms" he demands.
We have crossed from reality into some parallel universe where two grown men can speak to each other like this. I sit there in silence for a few beats, doing some internal calculations. I am working as a non-training grade, meaning I have no support network or anyone to intervene here. I can see no way I can continue working under Dr Spitzer safely or happily. So I made a decision. I stand up and walk out. I walk straight into the clinical lead's office two doors along and hand in my notice, and I walk back into an icy winter's night, raging, upset and slightly bewildered.

**

Why did I tell you this story? It certainly wasn't to recommend this course of action. Looking back, slightly older slightly wiser, I would not have done things the same. So why? I think to make the simple point that your doctors and nurses are just people too. They aren't always heroes and angels, they are all struggling under intense pressure and we are all fallible, myself included. We go through a lot of training to help make teams cohesive, to make sure different people can work together in the interest of their patient. But this doesn't always work.
Medicine is an extremely personal endeavour. If it's more of an art than a science, then there are perhaps a few too many artists rather than scientists. It's personal by its very nature, by the relationship you have with your patient, a fellow human being, and by how the hierarchy is arranged. You make a decision and it's yours alone, you take personal responsibility.
It really isn't any wonder that those personalities might clash sometimes. It's another barrier and pressure to good patient care, and something I am still only now learning to navigate. I honestly feel these things can be surmounted with simple gestures, like genuinely getting to know your team. Perhaps if Dr Spitzer and I had sat down over that coffee instead things might've gone differently.

**

Morale is at an all-time low in the NHS, and doubly so amongst its junior doctors. An NHS stretched beyond breaking point, in a resource-low and lawsuit-high environment has made medicine an increasingly less attractive career. The UK already has some of the fewest doctors per capita of population compared to our international peers.[75]

"Rota gaps" where a doctor should be in post but simply isn't are everywhere. Two out of three hospital trusts have at least one doctor missing per rotation. Despite promises to recruit more, in areas like GP for example the numbers are still falling. The number of junior doctors applying to go and work overseas has skyrocketed. The doctors of tomorrow will face innumerable challenges. What sort of workplace will they start in? Will there still be an NHS? Will we still respect, in any shape or form, the importance of "coffee?"

[75] Moberly T. UK has fewer doctors per person than most other OECD countries. BMJ [Internet]. 2017 Jun 20 [cited 2020 Feb 13];357.

Cortisol

It's the coldest day in December. I've been a doctor for six years. Snow is settling on the cars and ambulances parked bumper-to-bumper outside my A&E. Inside the corridors are lined with trolleys, some stacked side by side, the sick, frail and elderly lie in what feels like an endless queue. It feels like a natural disaster has happened somewhere; a freak storm, an earthquake, a meteor strike. Where have all these people come from? My bleep goes off for the thousandth time that evening, and then again before I can even reach the phone to answer the first. How can we cope? How did it get like this?

**

It's a warm spring day in March 2013. It's my first spring as a doctor. The sudden hot weather has caught the hospital by surprise and the ward is sweltering. I'm already sweating as I run down to A&E, carrying an urgent blood result from the acute medical ward. On my way back, I recognise a nurse I know looking distraught. Nick just qualified, he's six foot two, glasses and curly blonde hair, conscientious, thorough, polite, thoughtful. He looks as if he's been beaten. Catching my eye, he collars me.

"Dom. Please come and see these patients." He gestures behind him, through a dilapidated wooden door I always thought led to the old physiotherapy gym.

I scoff. "What patients? There's no ward down here."

Nick just walks off, gesturing for me to follow.

"There is now."

Beyond is what looks like a makeshift disaster relief zone. Ancient hospital trolleys from the seventies are lined up six deep in two opposing rows, separated by wheelie office partitions. A few oxygen cylinders and a computer on a fold-out desk make the "ward" complete. They haven't even removed all of the old gym equipment - a couple of exercise balls are still lurking in the corner.

"What is this?" I ask, slightly aghast this existed without my knowledge. "Which team is covering?"

"It's the "overflow" ward" Nick explains somewhat desperately. "And it's just me." He looks forlorn.

"Which doctors?" I ask.

"Well there's you now". Nick looks momentarily embarrassed, but then someone calls for him and he's off again.

I am bewildered. How can this be here and no one has responsibility for it? We had seen a massive surge in admissions since another A&E had closed a week prior. But it was the middle of spring - why did it look like the middle of winter already?

As one of my blunter colleagues put it; "As one A&E closes, another one is f****d."

I set about seeing the patients, my bleep buzzing angrily as my regular ward wondered where I'd got to. Some patients were very well, waiting for home or social care. Some were far sicker. An elderly lady had been admitted with weight loss and a high heart rate. She was emaciated with bulging wild eyes that made her look manic. In retrospect the diagnosis was literally staring me in the face, but at the time I was too stressed and too inexperienced to work it out. I knew she was sick but not why. My registrar later that day would diagnose her with Graves' disease, a life threatening thyroid condition, and she would end up being in hospital for three weeks.

Another gentleman looked haggard, cheeks flushed with the effort of drawing each breath, lips a lurid tint of dark purple. He was gasping desperately through a mask attached to an oxygen cylinder.

"How much oxygen is he on?" I asked Nick, bewildered he could be down here in this "discharge" ward.

Nick looked worried. "Ten litres." He nudged the cylinder with his foot, "that's not going to last much longer". This man ended up in Intensive Care. Fortunately, he survived.

Later I sat down with my medical registrar, Meera. Trained in Delhi, she was the only doctor I knew who seemed to have forgotten not a single iota of her medical school knowledge. I once asked her about the stress hormone, cortisol, and while she delivered a flawless textbook answer, she idly drew its molecular structure on a napkin.

Frustrated, bewildered, furious this ward had no assigned staff, I needed to vent.

"What happened?" I asked. "Why do we need a winter overflow ward in March?"

Meera gave me a look.

"It's always winter now."

**

Flash forward four years and I'm the registrar for medical admissions at one of the busiest hospitals in the country. One third of hospital trusts will go on to declare a "black alert" this winter, a status officially declared when a hospital feels activity exceeds its capacity to manage it safely. This hospital will spend more time at this level than any other in the U.K. The Red Cross will label this winter a "humanitarian crisis" in the NHS.[76]

On the frontline, that's what it feels like. The shift is relentless. The morning starts with a young man in his thirties fighting an aggressive lung cancer. He comes in with chest pain and a heart rate of nearly two hundred. He looks really sick. I set up shop in resuscitation with this patient; as I assess and treat him I deal with the admin of running the admissions team. Answering my bleep, reviewing the junior's notes, getting the consultant to see, a large percentage of the job is more managerial than medicine, and I have to bend backwards to keep both plates spinning. I do a bedside scan that shows his heart is trapped in a bubble of fluid larger than the heart itself, and it's starting to squeeze the life out of it. This is a possibly fatal emergency. Even as I'm doing this the morning consultant attempts to pull me away to talk about another junior. In a life-threatening condition I arrange to transfer the patient for a surgical drain at another hospital.

While I'm sorting that out, ten more patients are seen by various members of my team.

It's 11am. A middle-aged man staggers into the emergency department with his second heart attack in three months. He too needs an urgent transfer elsewhere. On route to see him the doors erupt with a paramedic team pushing in a woman in her seventies who collapsed suddenly at home, falling down the stairs. Her electrical heart tracing shows her heart intermittently stops beating entirely. She is rushed urgently for a pacemaker. I return to the ED to arrange the transfer for the man with the heart attack. I still haven't reviewed the ten patients from this morning, and by now ten more patients have been added to the list. Two consultants are doing rounds of their patients and I can't make it to either.

[76] Campbell D, Morris S, Marsh S. NHS faces 'humanitarian crisis' as demand rises, British Red Cross warns. The Guardian [Internet]. 2017 Jan 6 [cited 2020 Feb 14];

It's already chaos and its only just past midday. A GP phones me to admit a patient with end stage ovarian cancer and failing kidneys. Before I can ask any more questions I'm called to see a young man found collapsed at his work. He has sustained a head injury and bleed in his brain. I go to liaise with the surgical team to get an urgent opinion only to find my heart attack patient still hasn't been transferred. I go out to see if I can find what the ambulance delay is and help them prioritise. I bump into two of my junior doctors who discuss their cases with me. Both sound complex and I offer them advice, but I can't see their patients just yet.

It's 2pm and I check the medical list; five more patients have been seen by the junior team. I have no idea what is happening with them. I get a call from the site manager of the hospital: they need me to do a ward round for the "decisions unit" as they have no doctor there at the moment. I ask my consultant, who tells me that there should be someone and she will find out.

I go back to the acute admissions control room and my crash bleep goes off, I sprint up to the ward and find a frail 91-year-old lady collapsed with no blood pressure at all. We squeeze fluid into her and she makes a good recovery. I prescribe her antibiotics. She's looking better, but I've lost forty minutes I didn't have. I come down to A&E again to find ten more patients waiting and my team disappearing; it's 4pm and the shifts are changing.

I spot my man with a heart attack sitting in an open bay, clutching his chest. Angry now, I pick up the phone and call the ambulance service and then the heart team at our cardiac hospital. I make sure I see him loaded into the ambulance before I get back, but I shouldn't have had to. People are so easily lost down here.

I look around the heaving department and everywhere I see something I still need to do. As a student I worked for many years as a waiter in a busy American-themed restaurant. I even wore a cowboy hat. I'd spend eight hour shifts running back and forth between tables, bar and kitchen, dealing with angry customers and pressured managers and seemingly never coming up for air. This feels like I'm right back there again, to the tune of endless Johnny Cash on repeat, only the stakes are so much higher.

It's 5.30pm and the site manager calls me again. They still need a ward round on the 'decisions unit', no one ever came to make a decision. Swearing I rush round there, belligerently going through each patient case with the nurse, doing quick reviews to safely tide over the patients till the next day. It's far from ideal. I'm not making these patients better or closer to home, I'm just doing what I can until things can be sorted out tomorrow. It's all just playing catch up. I fear every day is like this.

Halfway through my bleep goes off; a surgical doctor is concerned his patient has become paralysed from the waist down. I rush up there and see the gentleman, a 45-year-old man who has been increasingly immobile for a month and now can't move his legs at all. I try and take the history and be as considerate as I can but my bleep interrupts us three times. I make a preliminary plan and arrange a Neurology opinion for the morning before rushing back downstairs.

It's evening time. Ten more patients on the list, forty plus I haven't seen. I try and quickly collar each of the more junior doctors to run through their patients. I stop when I bump into my most junior team member, Beth. Beth is a brand new doctor in her fourth month of working. She's Scottish, quiet, very knowledgeable and sensible. She looks upset.

"What is it?" I ask.

It transpires the GP patient with ovarian cancer has arrived and Beth is very worried. I listen to the history and stop when I see a pale emaciated lady in her sixties, lying on a trolley in a hospital corridor. Her family are gathered anxiously around her. I've been a doctor long enough to recognise when someone is close to the end.

It's nearly 8pm, handover time. I asked Beth to run the bleep to the new medical registrar and I set some time aside for this lady.

Margaret is 68, a piano teacher. She tells me weakly she would be still working if it weren't for the advanced cancer wracking her body. She's in a lot of pain. I flip through her notes: she's had three different types of chemotherapy already, and her oncologist has told her there's no further treatment left. I check her blood tests and find her kidneys are nearly completely shut down. She is dying.

The ED matron helps us get her into a side room, and Beth and I take some time to manage her symptoms. Pain relief, adjusted to her kidneys, and nausea medication. A drip for fluids. I glance at the ED clock. It's 9pm. I've missed the shift handover meeting entirely. I sigh.

This lady has made no decision about resuscitation. I know she could pass away tonight, and if I don't discuss this now with her she might end up dying an undignified and painful death. I broach the subject, but Margaret is well ahead of me.

"None of that" she says in a thick Yorkshire accent. "I don't want any heroics, none of that. Let me go quietly."

She grimaces in pain and just nods as I explain to her the process. We sign the form next to her. She grabs my wrist. "Let my family know. Please"

Outside her two grown up daughters and husband wait patiently. It's clear they all understand how sick she is. I try to find a quiet space to talk, but there simply isn't one anywhere in the department. I usher them into the only space not filled with people, the entryway to the linen cupboard. I squirm at how poor a part I am playing in this family's story. I long for the space and time to do this properly, like I would want a doctor to treat me and my family. Any of our families. But I can't. I explain as best I can the situation, her imminent likelihood of death, the order to not resuscitate. I answer their questions. They seem satisfied but I can't forgive myself.

I trudge back to the handover room and find the night registrar already inundated. We try to talk about the patient list, but I find I know very little about the sixty patients I admitted to hospital today. I feel like I'm not enough, like I've failed. Like two of me wouldn't be enough.

On the drive home that night I happened to catch a late night talk show hosting a phone in about NHS pressures in the emergency department. The host claims that all of the problems are because of drunks and foreigners. Margaret still in the back of my mind, lying on that trolley in an open hospital corridor, I see red.

I screech the car onto the hard shoulder and furiously dial into the program. The first doctor to call, they put me straight through. In my mind I put the radio show host's ridiculous claims down, pointing to my twelve hour shift and sixty sick frail and elderly patients on my list today - no drunks or foreigners, just the most vulnerable in our society suffering because of deep and savage underfunding of our services. At least that's what I tried to say. It probably came across as an incoherent furious rant and I got cut off before I swore too much. Still furious, deliriously tired, I pull back into the dual carriageway to drive home, and nearly crash my car into an oncoming van. It swerves and beeps and drives on.

My heart in my chest I come off again, get out of the car and calm down. It's nearly midnight, the roadside is freezing. I watch my breath mist in front of me. I'm twenty minutes away from my house. I get back in and drive very slowly and carefully home. Closing my front door very quietly so as not to wake my wife or three month-old daughter, I swear to myself to never drive after a long on-call shift again.

The next day is exactly the same.

**

When a human body deals with stress there are two main mechanisms that dictate how we respond. The first is driven by adrenaline, the hormone equivalent of nitrous oxide for the body - the heart beats quicker, the blood pressure rockets, your eyes let in more light, your muscles surge with energy. This is the 'fight or flight' response[77], and lasts minutes to hours.

The second is slower acting, it primes the body for long term stress situations. This is cortisol. It's made in glands just above both kidneys and it boosts the fluid you retain, breaks down muscle for extra energy, sustains you in the short term. But in the long term chronic cortisol release is incredibly toxic: you gain weight and change the fat composition in your body, your bones and muscles break down, you retain salt and fluid to a dangerously high degree.

The UK healthcare system has been under ever increasing pressure. There has been a lot of creative accounting and spin to explain away where that pressure comes from, but it's really very simple. Each year the activity in the NHS and its consequent cost rises above fiscal inflation, this is known as "health inflation." To understand why health costs rises year on year requires condensing the entire system into a single person. Let's call her Beverley.

Beverley, like the NHS, was born in 1948. Her birth is at home, with no healthcare professional, midwife or monitoring. Several of Beverley's siblings are also born this way, unfortunately two die before they are one. Sadly, an uncle has a heart attack at 52 and passes away.

Beverley grows up, and fortunately remains healthy. She marries Bob, and she has her kids in 1968. She has every one in a hospital, with a midwife. One requires surgery. Beverley's own mother has a stroke and dies at 63. Bob decides to stop smoking.

Beverley gets older. Her first grandchild is born in 1988, in hospital with electronic monitoring and emergency caesarean. Beverley's second grandchild is born at 25 weeks, and spends three months in the new intensive care baby unit. Stressed grandparent Bob has a heart attack, he is rushed into hospital and has an emergency procedure to open the blood vessels in his heart. He is at home in time to hold his new granddaughter for the first time.

Beverley and Bob stride on, both retiring at 65. On their 50th wedding anniversary Beverley feels odd, can't find the words to toast, and can't raise her left arm. Her daughter dials 999, Beverley has a stroke, just like her mother. Fortunately, she gets to hospital and 30 minutes later she has had a brain scan and a clot buster is being infused into her arm. She makes a full recovery, and goes back home a day later.

---

[77] Goldstein DS. Adrenal Responses to Stress. Cell Mol Neurobiol. 2010;30(8):1433–40.

The junior doctor looking after Beverley spots a shadow on the routine chest X-ray she has. She is diagnosed with lung cancer. Bob is going spare. They meet the specialist, the cancer is treatable and they start right away, six rounds of radiotherapy then weekly chemotherapy. It's hard, and Beverley goes into hospital twice with complications.

Halfway through Bob has lots of abdominal pain and throws up some blood. Rushed to hospital he has an emergency camera test into his stomach – he's developed a stress ulcer, which they clip and repair. He's in hospital for a few days. Gratefully Bob and Beverley return home.

Beverley goes into remission, but is very frail now and is falling a lot at home. Now in their eighties, Bob gets chest pain trying to look after them both, and Bob needs three more stents put in to open blocked heart vessels. Bob and Beverley ask for some social services support at home, a carer comes once a day.

One night Bob passes away in his sleep. Beverley is distraught, but at the funeral she asks her daughter; "Where's Bob?". Concerned, her daughter takes her to the GP. It's clear Beverley now has dementia. She is moved first to a sheltered flat, then a residential home, then a nursing home. She dies in hospital of a severe pneumonia at 83.

This isn't a sad story, this is modern life and modern healthcare.

Healthcare has changed. In 1948 the average female life expectancy was 71. Now it's over 81. Beverley's mum died at 63, while Beverley lived into her 80s. People are living longer. Why? Better healthcare, better immunisations and disease prevention, better nutrition certainly, but also diseases that were previously fatal are now treatable. Mortality for conditions such as heart attacks have halved in fifty years- Beverley's uncle died of a heart attack, but Bob survived two. Strokes and stomach bleeds are now mostly survivable whereas fifty years ago they were not.

However, these treatments are very expensive, the technology to open blood clots through vessels is super high tech and costs thousands per procedure, advanced chemotherapy and radiotherapy treatment costs can run to hundreds of thousands per person, and intensive baby care costs tens of thousands a week. In short, we can do more every year, so we do. Those that we save live on as survivors but this comes at a cost.

The cost of healthcare per year for an 85-year old is around twice that of a 65-year old and eight times that of a twenty year old[78]. The proportion of the UK population over 65 will increase by 60% over the next two decades.[79]

---

[78] Robineau D, Louter D. How much have I cost the NHS? [Internet]. the Guardian. [cited 2020 Feb 14].

[79] Kingston A, Comas-Herrera A, Jagger C. Forecasting the care needs of the older population in England over the next 20 years: estimates from the Population Ageing and Care Simulation (PACSim) modelling study. Lancet Public Health. 2018 Aug 31;3(9):e447–55.

So more people, who need more treatment, are treated with more medicines and survive more to need more treatment in the future, as well as more social care. Tack on staff wage inflation, increasing technology and drug costs as treatment gets ever more advanced and you will now see why the healthcare systems need a 3-4% rise in funding every year[80]. Every industrialised country in the world is exactly the same.

**

As I'm standing in the emergency department today, watching ambulance crews backing up with their patients in their tens, watching intensive care patients stuck in emergency beds because they have nowhere to transfer to, watching palliative care and mental health patients stuck waiting for placements hundreds of miles away, I can't help but think we haven't met that rising demand. Nowhere near. We aren't coping with the stress, and it's wearing down the services and the staff.

It cannot come as a surprise to the government that the healthcare system experiences annual increases in demand - this has been the case for the past seventy years. Year-on-year the mismatch between funding and demand has been building, and now the deficit is snowballing[81]. The pressure, the stress, the cortisol is killing the service.

Across every metric of healthcare performance, waiting times, the fiscal deficit, staffing numbers, we are in deep trouble. Despite the warnings and the publicised battles with the government, the constant stream of front cover news stories of the NHS crisis, nowhere near enough has been done.

If the NHS were a patient, I would be pulling the alarm cord right about now. In a way I suppose I am. We all are.

---

[80] How hospital activity in the NHS in England has changed over time [Internet]. The King's Fund. 2016 [cited 2020 Feb 14].

[81] How is the NHS performing? July 2019 quarterly monitoring report [Internet]. The King's Fund. 2019 [cited 2020 Feb 14].

Larynx

The January gales spatter icy drops across the pane of my clinic window. I'm sitting with Wallace, a softly-spoken retired gardener in his late seventies, who has come to the cardiology clinic today with a short history of what sounds very much like angina, pain from the heart due to a tight coronary artery. As we are running through his medicines, I briefly ask him about his allergies, and he starts telling me the strangest story I've heard for some time.

Twenty years' prior, Wallace had been working on a hot summer's day in a busy city park, and decided to treat himself to an ice cream, double chocolate with all the trimmings; fudge sauce, chocolate flake, sprinkles. He sat on a bench by the fountain in the blistering sun, taking the world in. Then he got back to work.

After about forty minutes, Wallace began to feel unwell; dizzy, light-headed. Switching off his power tools he sat down heavily and the next thing he knew he was waking up with a crowd of worried faces looking down at him. He'd passed out. He was taken to hospital, and after a battery of normal tests, a helpful doctor told him he "was allergic to chocolate" and he should avoid it. And so, for the last twenty years, after a life-long sweet tooth, poor Wallace had been teetotal to all cocoa-based confectionery goodies, through twenty Christmases, Birthdays and Easters.

I went back through this day two decades ago; he denied he had any lip or tongue swelling, rashes, itch or breathing difficulties. He didn't report any heart symptoms either; no palpitations or pains in the chest. He'd never had a problem with any chocolate prior to that, and he was adamant it was about an hour later that he fainted. Somehow what was nearly certainly a simple faint on a hot day had become labelled callously as a 'chocolate allergy' and never re-addressed.

I sit in silence for a moment, marvelling at the power our words have on our patients, and how incredibly careful we should be about it. At some point a doctor, at least as remembered by the patient, had made an off-hand comment that had irrevocably changed a man's entire life.

We talk about how this 'allergy' is very unlikely to be a true allergy, despite a third of Wallace's life believing it so, and how we could get him formally tested and then back on to chocolate once more. Even as I explain, Wallace then starts having more of the chest pains that had brought him to us in the first place. At rest now, these symptoms constitute an emergency, and we admit Wallace directly to a hospital bed. He has two stents to open up his heart arteries the next morning. Perhaps, in my haste to explain to Wallace his new freedom to enjoy chocolate again, I had forgotten the weight of my own words, precipitating his angina and emergency admission. As I keep having to remind myself, our words, all of our words, have power.

**

Interactions like Wallace's are commonplace. Despite the years of training, knowledge and procedural ability of doctors, the large majority of our job is simply listening and talking. A job we don't always get right. It's such an important part of being a doctor. Large swathes of the medical school curriculum are solely dedicated to just that; teaching the skills to listen, and to talk. How to 'actively' listen, how to prompt and when not to, how to fight the inner urge to interrupt. How to explain diagnosis, prognosis, the good news and the bad. And chief of all: the "doorknob" complaint. Hearkening back from the era when we still saw patients in offices, with doors and door knobs, the "doorknob" complaint is the problem the patient voices just as they are leaving, with their hand on the doorknob, and usually begins with "By the way..." or "just a quick question...". Invariably it is the most important symptom, and the one the patient is actually worried about. Sometimes, it's the question we never thought to ask at all.

**

It's Christmas Day, and I am finishing my core medical hospital rotations with a stint in oncology. Lumbered with the Christmas Eve night shift, it's actually 0130am and I am sitting feeling sorry for myself on the private ward, munching my way through the mountains of incredibly expensive gifted chocolates that always appear at this time of year. As the on-call oncology junior we cover emergencies and busy-work overnight on all the wards, including the private ward, where patients have flown across continents to receive some of the world's best cancer care. It can be quite stressful to attend emergencies here, where the patients are often outside of the usual systems and there's an entirely different day team. But tonight, the ward is thankfully quiet, and stocked with a Willy Wonka-level smorgasbord of artisanal chocolate. I've never seen anything like this before; all the chocolate brands are actual human names, like perfumes or fashion designers. I pick up a perfect glittering orb the size of a large marble, shrouded in heavy gold and embossed with something like "Indi Gottier"; inside is the world's fanciest Malteaser; covered in perfectly smooth milk chocolate flecked with real gold, the inside is a layer of another darker truffle over actual honeycomb. The nurses found me after I've eaten about six.

"Can you see Mr Okafor please? He's 'spiking' again" the ward sister says, even as her arched eyebrow and smirk say something else entirely.

"Of course! It's Christmas right?" I bounce up, slightly woozy from the sugar rush, and hare off to dig through Mr Okafor's notes.

'Spiking' is the term we use for a fever, a temperature over 38°C, and as I trace his trends over the last week or so I see Mr Okafor has been 'spiking' every two or three days. I read all his medical notes and flick through his bloods: in his mid-sixties, he has been unwell for about a month, his blood markers of inflammation are high, and no one seems to know why. The team seems to be thinking he might have a rare form of blood cancer, and he is awaiting more tests after the holiday. I add a prescription and then go and see him.

Mr Okafor is sitting up in bed, reading yesterday's papers. For his age, he seems fit and full of life. A face weathered with long laughter lines crinkles into a smile at my arrival.

"Hello Mr Okafor, I'm Dominic the night-doctor, how are you feeling?"

"Oh just fine doctor, just fine. Merry Christmas by the way"

"Merry Christmas, sir."

I go about and listen to heart and lungs. He feels hot, and close up there's a tenseness around his eyes suggesting he is far more worn out than he lets on, but otherwise I can't find much else to add.

"Well, we will keep going with the tests, and give you something for the fever." I say, halfway out the room myself.

"Oh good, oh good. Do you think I'll be home before New Year?" he asks, with my own hand on the doorknob.

"Oh, um, I'm not sure." I really have no idea what his diagnosis is, it's 0130am in the morning, and if he does have leukaemia or myeloma he will be in hospital for weeks starting treatment. At least. I decide to divert. "Where's home for you Mr Okafor?"

"Lagos! That's in Nigeria you know." I did know, but it got me thinking.

"Oh really? When were you last there?"

"Oh just two weeks ago. Went to the hospital there and then flew straight here, my family checked me in." Suddenly alarm bells are going off in my head.

"Have you ever had something called malaria, Mr Okafor?"

"Of course! Many times. I was in hospital in Lagos with malaria just before I came here."

"You mean a few weeks ago."

"Yes".

"Did you ever mention this?"

"No one ever asked!"

I go back through his notes – nowhere is it mentioned he had so recently been in Lagos, where chronic and acute malaria is nearly as common as a cold, and nowhere is it mentioned he had been diagnosed with malaria already.

In the morning we send his malaria films, and sure enough in one slide of his blood film is a tiny malarial parasite waving back at us. A few days of a new antimalarial and Mr Okafor was discharged home. The right words spoken at the right time can make all the difference.

**

When it comes down to it, words are pretty much the entirety of our jobs. Some of the hardest moments in my career have been struggling to find the right ones. Telling a roomful of loved ones how their mother/sister/wife unexpectedly passed away. Trying to explain to a dying man's relatives that there were no more treatments for his heart failure left to us, having the same conversation at 2am with a tearful wife beyond her wits end. Finding the words to comfort the junior nurse reduced to tears by the same situation. After these sometimes hours of talking, we go and write them all down in documents that often end up hundreds of pages long. The most important lesson I'm still learning as a doctor is what to say and what not to say, and when.

The science of speech is fascinating. The seat of all expression, good or bad, every kind word or ill, every hateful curse or tender blessing, is centimetre sized organ that sits at the base of the throat. Speech is generated by passing air expelled from the lungs across two stretched pieces of tissue, the vocal cords.[82] Through fine vibrations of this V shaped apparatus, coupled with secondary generators of speech in the tongue and lips, we can speak, orate, vocalise, chat, scald, repudiate, admonish, compliment, or praise. Our voices are extremely important. They are our imprint on the world. In many ways our voices are the only true external representation of ourselves.

As a professional body of doctors we aren't known for being particularly vocal. Our practice is mostly about listening. We are consciously taught to cut away bias and prejudice and consequently our professional code of conduct is to not express our own opinions. However, there are rare times when that code demands that we speak up.

**

It's 2016, a freezing day in January, and I'm huddled behind an eight-foot blown-up cover of "How To Read A Paper", a statistics manual for beginners, hoping an icy gust doesn't blow it down before we reach the crowd of press and photographers twenty yards ahead. A group of around ten of us, junior doctors all, in scrubs and civilian clothes and joined by several notable professors, start marching down the length of Whitehall. We have a message for the Secretary of State for Health, the Rt. Hon Jeremy Hunt.

**

The phrase "junior doctor" only fully emerged into public consciousness with the junior doctor strike action in 2016[83]. It feels impossible to fully encapsulate exactly why thousands of doctors would go on all out strike for the first time in UK history, but essentially many felt the new contract the government proposed for junior doctors was punitive and unsafe, remaining a predominantly cost-cutting measure.

---

[82] Isshiki N. Physiology of Speech Production. In: Isshiki N, editor. Phonosurgery: Theory and Practice [Internet]. Tokyo: Springer Japan; 1989 [cited 2020 Feb 14]. p. 5–21.

[83] Junior doctors' row: The dispute explained. BBC News [Internet]. 2016 Apr 6 [cited 2020 Feb 14]; Available from: https://www.bbc.com/news/health-34775980

The words the Health Secretary of the time used inflamed the situation to an unprecedented level of escalation. He claimed hospitals were unsafe at the weekends, based on fairly dubious evidence. Worse still, the national furore over this "weekend effect" and its echo in the right wing press led to a widespread belief hospitals are unsafe at weekends. Evidence of patients delaying treatment in life-threatening conditions, such as stroke, due to stoked fears over the "weekend effect" was given its own term, the "Hunt effect". His words had real and lasting harm up and down the country.

Many, like myself, felt the level of misinformation and misconceptions about the health service in general was reaching a dangerous degree, with patient harm as a consequence. Through the early protests and then the strikes and beyond I was absorbed by the effort to try and correct the narrative, to try and fight the imposition of what we saw as a dangerous contract. Like many others it stretched my morale beyond breaking point, and poisoned my love for my job and the service. Worse, it put a strain on my marriage, I lost perspective of the time I was spending away from home, never present even when I was; on Twitter, or my blog, or planning the next stunt or protest. I even wrote a five-thousand-word treatise on a government debate about the contract on our honeymoon. I was obsessed. I never really apologised to my wife. I'm truly sorry.

By the end of that year I felt exhausted, demoralised, and directionless. The only thing I knew for sure was I had to be there for my wife and soon-to-be daughter. I quit my training job, closed my blog, and walked away. Despite all our words and protests, we had failed.

**

A year later, I am sitting in the third row, left of centre, in a lecture theatre at the Royal Society of Medicine. Ten feet away from me is the world's most famous academic, Professor Stephen Hawking. He is giving a speech on his struggle with motor neurone disease and the medical care he received in the NHS. Between each sentence the room sits in rapt silence, the only noise the quiet beeps and clicks of Professor Hawking's on-board computer.

He recounts the history of his life-changing illness. From a healthy young man slowly his muscles began to fail him. First the muscles of his legs, leaving him in a wheelchair, then his arms, then his throat affecting his ability to swallow safely, requiring a tracheostomy, a tube in the windpipe that cut off the air flow through the larynx and removed his ability to speak entirely. What was remarkable and inspiring is none of this stopped him, despite being told he would die within days, not once, but three times, he lived on to become one of the foremost physicists in the world. He never gave up. He spoke for just under an hour, about the NHS, about Jeremy Hunt, about the "weekend effect"[84]. I could almost convince myself at one point he paraphrased an article of mine. My words, spoken by one of the greatest minds of our generation. The idea was mad, but it was enough to inspire me back to write again. My voice was important, as all our voices are. Words can change the world.

His intervention, a public condemnation, made headlines around the world. This speech very sadly would be one of his last. He passed away not soon after. His genius and resilience was only matched by his incredible humanity, a humanity that truly touched millions of lives, mine included. May he rest in peace.

**

In many ways I have a lot to thank Jeremy Hunt for. It's only when you're about to lose something that you see it's truest value. My job, my family, our NHS. Walking away from my job as a doctor made me re-evaluate why I chose to become a doctor in the first place, made me rediscover my love for it and come back again. My choice to prioritise my family, to put my wife and children ahead of all else, taught me what is genuinely important in life. Lastly I have never seen more clearly the inherent value of our NHS.

---

[84] Stephen Hawking responds to Jeremy Hunt and it's savage [Internet]. indy100. 2017 [cited 2020 Feb 14].

Working as a doctor is an incredible privilege but one that carries a heavy burden of responsibility. Healthcare professionals have a duty of care, enshrined in law, to speak up for our patients, to warn them, to help them make informed decisions. So many of us have been speaking out against the damage we are seeing to people's lives, warning of the precarious future that lies ahead. Trying to share the genuine reality of life inside our precious NHS as best we can. Informed consent is the bedrock of medicine; my job as a doctor is to give you all the information to the best of my ability, and then, after weighing each risk and benefit, you decide what's best for you. So now that you may consider yourself "informed", the question remains. What are you going to do about it?

END

Addendum/Adrenaline

It's about 6 months after I finished the first draft of this book and I have returned to training in a tertiary emergency Cardiology hospital.
I've been here for just four days, I'm on call, it's a quiet Sunday afternoon. I take a sip of coffee and flick through a patient's blood results.

**

Two miles away Jasper is flicking idly through the sports pages of the Mail. In his late forties, slightly overweight and a heavy smoker, Jasper hasn't ever had a medical problem before. Until now.
He grabs his chest in sudden agony, shooting heavy pain that grips his left arm and jaw. Sweaty and clammy he calls for his son to call an ambulance.

**

I finish up checking the last results and then I pull a big stack of clinic letters to approve. I take another sip of coffee.

**

The ambulance crew take the stairs up to Jasper's flat two at a time, take a quick history and give him a spray of medication to stabilise him as they stick electrodes to his chest and run a portable ECG. Jasper is having a massive heart attack. They put the call out.

**

My bleep alarms and rattles on the desk and then squawks;
"PRIMARY ANGIOPLASTY. Confirmed anterior MI. Arrival five minutes"
My heart plummets as I bolt out of the ward and rush down ten flights of stairs to the heart attack centre. This is what I've been dreading.

**

In recent years, the emergency management of heart attack has changed dramatically. Paramedic crews trained to recognise serious and near fatal myocardial infarction now bypass the entire hospital and bring those patients immediately to the cardiologist's front door. We have a target of 90 minutes[85] from arrival at hospital to a life-saving procedure called percutaneous coronary intervention (PCI) where we thread a balloon millimetres wide on the end of a wire through the arteries and into the heart itself. We call this "door to balloon" time.

It's one of the most revolutionary techniques of the past twenty years and saves thousands of lives in the UK every year. It's also extremely technical and, at least at first, incredibly terrifying to perform.

**

As Jasper hurtles towards us in the back of an ambulance his vital signs are starting to teeter. I'm scrambling around the cardiac laboratory trying to get the kit ready, call the consultant and cajole the lab team all at once. I've only done this only a handful of times and my hands are shaking. My role is to assist, to hand things across and receive instruments from the consultant. It's such a minor role. Yet my heart won't stop thumping out of my chest.

Jasper makes land, screeching to a stop at the heart attack service door as the paramedic crew rush him in. I snatch the ECG and feel my heartbeat climb further, whooshing in my ears. I'd hoped there'd been a mistake, that this wasn't a heart attack at all, but the electrical tracings show me quite the opposite. In fact, it's so abnormal we even have a colloquial name for its appearance, given both for the shape of the ECG pattern and its great risk of death; we call it "tombstoning".

I quickly look Jasper over. He's in agony, his blood pressure is low and he looks moribund. I give him some heart medications and super strong pain relief and call the consultant again as I scurry into the lab.

The consultant hears the story and is already en route. He reels off a bunch of technical descriptors I barely catch. I haplessly try to relay that to the nurse who has already got all the right kit ready. All of my career whenever I've been hopelessly out of my depth the nurses have saved me. Every doctor will tell you the same. We don't thank them nearly enough.

---

85 Door to balloon times for STEMI [Internet]. BCIS. [cited 2020 Feb 14].

The consultant Dr Normandy sweeps in, scrubbed in seconds and then standing next to me. Jasper is half draped, the instruments aren't entirely ready, the rapidity of the situation has outpaced me. I feel a failure. Dr Normandy doesn't stop for a beat; he whirs through noiselessly. Swipe to the skin to sterilise, swish of the drapes, touch to the skin and then pop, the first puncture to the artery releases a whisper thin jet of blood that spurts across at me. The needle is threaded with a wire, then a sheath, and then a long tube is passed through the whole thing. Dr Normandy can't have been in the room for longer than three minutes and he now has an instrument inside Jasper's heart.

Jasper is in a bad way. He's become delirious and is thrashing around under the table. We give him a little sedation and a lot more pain relief but it's something else. A moment later his heart tracing disappears into a storm of wild electricity, his heart has stopped beating.

Dr Normandy breaks his silence: "Shock please"

One of the radiographers' rushes around the bed. Even in my frenetic state I know enough to snatch my hands off the table. Just in time as Jasper convulses and then drops back again. No response.

"Shock again. Crash call". Dr Normandy's voice is like steel wire. Jasper spasms once more. His heart tracing flips into an ordered lub dub. He's alive.

Dr Normandy doesn't stop for a second. His hands are straight back on the instruments so quickly I wonder if he ever put them down. He shoots some dye down the tube and the coronary arteries suddenly appear on the x-ray screens in front of us, one artery is entirely blocked at its origin, it looks like a stump. Dr Normandy whips out one tube and threads two more in its place. A balloon and a wire. He inflates the balloon inside the heart vessel and checks the flow. The blockage is gone; the artery is flowing normally.

He sighs heavily.

"And now we relax." He gives a chuckle.

Jasper is sleeping peacefully and all his vitals are normalising.

Dr Normandy turns to me.

"Oh hi Dom. How are you doing? Alright?"

I'm twitching with adrenaline, panting with fear, sweating through my scrubs and lead overcoat, and still praying Jasper is going to wake up.

"Yeah, I'm okay". I squeak.

Dr Normandy just chuckles again and calmly finishes saving Jasper's life.

**

A few hours later I pop up to the ward to find Jasper sitting up in bed, pain free, eating a hospital chicken korma and watching Strictly Come Dancing on his bedside television.

"How are you doing Jasper?"

"I'm okay doc. Bit of pain."

"Oh that's okay" I reply." "It's normal to have some chest pain after a procedure like that, and we did have to shock the heart as well."

"No not my chest." Jasper looks at me like I'm being thick. "My tooth. Right here."

He opens his jaw wide and points to a slightly browned molar at the back of his mouth.

"Um. You probably need to see a dentist for that."

"Oh okay. Righto." Jasper turns back to his TV. I wander away, slightly overwhelmed. This man was dead three hours ago. Now his biggest concern is a sore tooth. As the adrenaline wears off a euphoria seeps in. I find myself laughing and crying with joy and can't seem to stop.

This is the best job in the world.

End.
(Really).

Acknowledgements

To my sister, for never letting me give up.

To my Dad, for filling our house with books and showing me it was possible to do anything.

To Rob & Grace (mostly Grace) for your kind words and insightful edits!

To Emily, for the same.

To Henry, for making me believe this was possible.

To Dilsan, for everything, for always.

To everybody else I harassed and emailed for thoughts and reviews, Ben and Rachel, Eime and Sarah - thank you for indulging me.

And to all the patients I have had the privilege of knowing and caring for. You taught me as much about medicine as about life itself.

Bibliography (Alphabetical)

1.

1918 Pandemic (H1N1 virus) | Pandemic Influenza (Flu) | CDC [Internet]. 2019 [cited 2020 Feb 12]. Available from: https://www.cdc.gov/flu/pandemic-resources/1918-pandemic-h1n1.html

2.

1000 Genomes Project Consortium, Auton A, Brooks LD, Durbin RM, Garrison EP, Kang HM, et al. A global reference for human genetic variation. Nature. 2015 Oct 1;526(7571):68–74.

3.

Perkins GD, Ji C, Deakin CD, Quinn T, Nolan JP, Scomparin C, et al. A Randomized Trial of Epinephrine in Out-of-Hospital Cardiac Arrest. New England Journal of Medicine. 2018 Aug 23;379(8):711–21.

4.

Goldstein DS. Adrenal Responses to Stress. Cell Mol Neurobiol. 2010;30(8):1433–40.

5.

Chisolm-Straker M, Cherkas D. Altered and unstable: wet beriberi, a clinical review. J Emerg Med. 2013 Sep;45(3):341–4.

6.

Bianconi E, Piovesan A, Facchin F, Beraudi A, Casadei R, Frabetti F, et al. An estimation of the number of cells in the human body. Ann Hum Biol. 2013 Dec;40(6):463–71.

7.

Aslam B, Wang W, Arshad MI, Khurshid M, Muzammil S, Rasool MH, et al. Antibiotic resistance: a rundown of a global crisis. Infect Drug Resist. 2018 Oct 10;11:1645–58.

8.

Unemo M, Shafer WM. Antimicrobial Resistance in Neisseria gonorrhoeae in the 21st Century: Past, Evolution, and Future. Clin Microbiol Rev. 2014 Jul;27(3):587–613.

9.

CLARKE E, STANNARD J. Aristotle on the Anatomy of the Brain. Journal of the History of Medicine and Allied Sciences. 1963;18(2):130–48.

10.

Strnad M, Lešnik D, Križmarić M. Arterial blood gas changes during cardiac arrest and cardiopulmonary resuscitation combined with passive oxygenation/ventilation: a METI HPS study. J Int Med Res. 2018 Nov;46(11):4605–16.

11.

BBC One - Doctor Who, Series 6, The Doctor's Wife [Internet]. BBC. [cited 2020 Feb 13]. Available from: https://www.bbc.co.uk/programmes/b011884d

12.

Gawande A. Being Mortal: Illness, Medicine and What Matters in the End. Profile Books Ltd; 2015. 296 p.

13.

Janfaza S, Banan Nojavani M, Khorsand B, Nikkhah M, Zahiri J. Cancer Odor Database (COD): a critical databank for cancer diagnosis research. Database (Oxford) [Internet]. 2017 Aug 3 [cited 2020 Feb 12];2017. Available from: https://www.ncbi.nlm.nih.gov/pmc/articles/PMC5737198/

14.

Wilbert-Lampen U, Leistner D, Greven S, Pohl T, Sper S, Völker C, et al. Cardiovascular events during World Cup soccer. N Engl J Med. 2008 Jan 31;358(5):475–83.

15.

Rodríguez-Artalejo F, López-García E. Coffee Consumption and Cardiovascular Disease: A Condensed Review of Epidemiological Evidence and Mechanisms. J Agric Food Chem. 2018 May 30;66(21):5257–63.

16.

Milos G. Coffee's Mysterious Origins [Internet]. The Atlantic. 2010 [cited 2020 Feb 13]. Available from: https://www.theatlantic.com/health/archive/2010/08/coffees-mysterious-origins/61054/

17.

Dame Cicely Saunders, founder of the modern hospice movement, dies. BMJ [Internet]. 2020 Feb 6 [cited 2020 Feb 13]; Available from: https://www.bmj.com/content/suppl/2005/07/18/331.7509.DC1

18.

Door to balloon times for STEMI [Internet]. BCIS. [cited 2020 Feb 14]. Available from: https://www.bcis.org.uk/patient-area/door-balloon-times/

19.

O'Sullivan SS, Evans AH, Lees AJ. Dopamine dysregulation syndrome: an overview of its epidemiology, mechanisms and management. CNS Drugs. 2009;23(2):157–70.

20.

Maruthappu M, Watkins J, Noor AM, Williams C, Ali R, Sullivan R, et al. Economic downturns, universal health coverage, and cancer mortality in high-income and middle-income countries, 1990-2010: a longitudinal analysis. Lancet. 2016 Aug 13;388(10045):684–95.

21.

Killgore WDS. Effects of sleep deprivation on cognition. Prog Brain Res. 2010;185:105–29.

22.

Wunsch H, Scales D, Gershengorn HB, Hua M, Hill AD, Fu L, et al. End-of-Life Care Received by Physicians Compared With Nonphysicians. JAMA Network Open. 2019 Jul 24;2(7):e197650–e197650.

23.

Prasad R, Singh A, Balasubramanian V, Gupta N. Extensively drug-resistant tuberculosis in India: Current evidence on diagnosis & management. Indian J Med Res. 2017 Mar;145(3):271–93.

24.

Aggarwal A, Manrai M, Kochhar R. Fluid resuscitation in acute pancreatitis. World J Gastroenterol. 2014 Dec 28;20(48):18092–103.

25.

Kingston A, Comas-Herrera A, Jagger C. Forecasting the care needs of the older population in England over the next 20 years: estimates from the Population Ageing and Care Simulation (PACSim) modelling study. Lancet Public Health. 2018 Aug 31;3(9):e447–55.

26.

Di Chiara G, Morelli M, Acquas E, Carboni E. Functions of dopamine in the extrapyramidal and limbic systems. Clues for the mechanism of drug actions. Arzneimittelforschung. 1992 Feb;42(2A):231–7.

27.

Schiefsky M. Galen and the tripartite soul. In 2012. p. 331–49.

28.

Bowden R, MacFie TS, Myers S, Hellenthal G, Nerrienet E, Bontrop RE, et al. Genomic Tools for Evolution and Conservation in the Chimpanzee: Pan troglodytes ellioti Is a Genetically Distinct Population. PLOS Genetics. 2012 Mar 1;8(3):e1002504.

29.

How hospital activity in the NHS in England has changed over time [Internet]. The King's Fund. 2016 [cited 2020 Feb 14]. Available from: https://www.kingsfund.org.uk/publications/hospital-activity-funding-changes

30.

How is the NHS performing? July 2019 quarterly monitoring report [Internet]. The King's Fund. 2019 [cited 2020 Feb 14]. Available from: https://www.kingsfund.org.uk/publications/how-nhs-performing-july-2019

31.

Robineau D, Louter D. How much have I cost the NHS? [Internet]. the Guardian. [cited 2020 Feb 14]. Available from: http://www.theguardian.com/society/ng-interactive/2016/feb/08/how-much-have-i-cost-the-nhs

32.

Rutherford A. How to Argue With a Racist: What Our Genes Do (and Don't) Say About Human Difference. S.l.: The Experiment; 2020. 224 p.

33.

Walters S, Benitez-Majano S, Muller P, Coleman MP, Allemani C, Butler J, et al. Is England closing the international gap in cancer survival? Br J Cancer. 2015 Sep 1;113(5):848–60.

34.

Junior doctors' row: The dispute explained. BBC News [Internet]. 2016 Apr 6 [cited 2020 Feb 14]; Available from: https://www.bbc.com/news/health-34775980

35.

Ding Ming, Bhupathiraju Shilpa N., Satija Ambika, van Dam Rob M., Hu Frank B. Long-Term Coffee Consumption and Risk of Cardiovascular Disease. Circulation. 2014 Feb 11;129(6):643–59.

36.

Estroff TW. Manual of Adolescent Substance Abuse Treatment. American Psychiatric Publishing; 2008. 319 p.

37.

Lin JY, Fisher DE. Melanocyte biology and skin pigmentation. Nature. 2007 Feb 22;445(7130):843–50.

38.

Campbell D, Morris S, Marsh S. NHS faces 'humanitarian crisis' as demand rises, British Red Cross warns. The Guardian [Internet]. 2017 Jan 6 [cited 2020 Feb 14]; Available from: https://www.theguardian.com/society/2017/jan/06/nhs-faces-humanitarian-crisis-rising-demand-british-red-cross

39.

NIH Human Microbiome Project defines normal bacterial makeup of the body [Internet]. National Institutes of Health (NIH). 2015 [cited 2020 Feb 12]. Available from: https://www.nih.gov/news-events/news-releases/nih-human-microbiome-project-defines-normal-bacterial-makeup-body

40.

Menini A, Lagostena L, Boccaccio A. Olfaction: From Odorant Molecules to the Olfactory Cortex. Physiology. 2004 Jun 1;19(3):101–4.

41.

Piovesan A, Pelleri MC, Antonaros F, Strippoli P, Caracausi M, Vitale L. On the length, weight and GC content of the human genome. BMC Research Notes. 2019 Feb 27;12(1):106.

42.

Mahlknecht P, Pechlaner R, Boesveldt S, Volc D, Pinter B, Reiter E, et al. Optimizing odor identification testing as quick and accurate diagnostic tool for Parkinson's disease. Mov Disord. 2016;31(9):1408–13.

43.

Millard C, Wessely S. Parity of esteem between mental and physical health. BMJ [Internet]. 2014 Nov 14 [cited 2020 Feb 12];349. Available from: https://www.bmj.com/content/349/bmj.g6821

44.

Galvan A, Wichmann T. Pathophysiology of Parkinsonism. Clin Neurophysiol. 2008 Jul;119(7):1459–74.

45.

DE HERT M, CORRELL CU, BOBES J, CETKOVICH-BAKMAS M, COHEN D, ASAI I, et al. Physical illness in patients with severe mental disorders. I. Prevalence, impact of medications and disparities in health care. World Psychiatry. 2011 Feb;10(1):52–77.

46.

Isshiki N. Physiology of Speech Production. In: Isshiki N, editor. Phonosurgery: Theory and Practice [Internet]. Tokyo: Springer Japan; 1989 [cited 2020 Feb 14]. p. 5–21. Available from: https://doi.org/10.1007/978-4-431-68358-2_2

47.

Wang Y, Zhao S. Placental Blood Circulation [Internet]. Morgan & Claypool Life Sciences; 2010 [cited 2020 Feb 12]. Available from: https://www.ncbi.nlm.nih.gov/books/NBK53254/

48.

Hogan H, Healey F, Neale G, Thomson R, Vincent C, Black N. Preventable deaths due to problems in care in English acute hospitals: a retrospective case record review study. BMJ Qual Saf. 2012 Sep;21(9):737–45.

49.

Brindley PG, Olusanya S, Wong A, Crowe L, Hawryluck L. Psychological 'burnout' in healthcare professionals: Updating our understanding, and not making it worse. J Intensive Care Soc. 2019 Nov;20(4):358–62.

50.

Ramsay G, Haynes AB, Lipsitz SR, Solsky I, Leitch J, Gawande AA, et al. Reducing surgical mortality in Scotland by use of the WHO Surgical Safety Checklist. BJS (British Journal of Surgery). 2019 Jul 1;106(8):1005–11.

51.

Harris D, Willoughby H. Resuscitation on television: realistic or ridiculous? A quantitative observational analysis of the portrayal of cardiopulmonary resuscitation in television medical drama. Resuscitation. 2009 Nov;80(11):1275–9.

52.

Bijland LR, Bomers MK, Smulders YM. Smelling the diagnosis: a review on the use of scent in diagnosing disease. Neth J Med. 2013 Aug;71(6):300–7.

53.

Cambau E, Poljak M. Sniffing animals as a diagnostic tool in infectious diseases. Clin Microbiol Infect. 2019 Nov 14;

54.

Statistics » A&E Attendances and Emergency Admissions [Internet]. [cited 2020 Feb 12]. Available from: https://www.england.nhs.uk/statistics/statistical-work-areas/ae-waiting-times-and-activity/

55.

Statistics » Provider-based Cancer Waiting Times for December 2019 (Provisional) [Internet]. [cited 2020 Feb 13]. Available from: https://www.england.nhs.uk/statistics/statistical-work-areas/cancer-waiting-times/monthly-prov-cwt/2019-20-monthly-provider-cancer-waiting-times-statistics/provider-based-cancer-waiting-times-for-december-2019-provisional/

56.

Stephen Hawking responds to Jeremy Hunt and it's savage [Internet]. indy100. 2017 [cited 2020 Feb 14]. Available from: http://www.indy100.com/article/stephen-hawking-video-response-jeremy-hunt-nhs-seven-days-a-week-healthcare-7908111

57.

Quraishi MN, Widlak M, Bhala N, Moore D, Price M, Sharma N, et al. Systematic review with meta-analysis: the efficacy of faecal microbiota transplantation for the treatment of recurrent and refractory Clostridium difficile infection. Aliment Pharmacol Ther. 2017;46(5):479–93.

58.

Sealove BA, Tiyyagura S, Fuster V. Takotsubo cardiomyopathy. J Gen Intern Med. 2008 Nov;23(11):1904–8.

59.

Gawande A. The Checklist Manifesto: How to Get Things Right. Journal of Nursing Regulation. 2011 Jan 31;1:64.

60.

Plato P. The Complete Plato by Plato. 1819 p.

61.

The History of Coffee Began in a Tiny City You've Probably Never Heard Of [Internet]. Mic. [cited 2020 Feb 13]. Available from: https://www.mic.com/articles/91347/the-history-of-coffee-began-in-a-tiny-city-you-ve-probably-never-heard-of

62.

Hasleton PS. The internal surface area of the adult human lung. J Anat. 1972 Sep;112(Pt 3):391–400.

63.

Ochs M, Nyengaard JR, Jung A, Knudsen L, Voigt M, Wahlers T, et al. The Number of Alveoli in the Human Lung. Am J Respir Crit Care Med. 2004 Jan 1;169(1):120–4.

64.

Szabo G. The regional anatomy of the human integument with special reference to the distribution of hair follicles, sweat glands and melanocytes. Philosophical Transactions of the Royal Society of London Series B, Biological Sciences. 1967 Sep 22;252(779):447–85.

65.

Fitzpatrick TB. The validity and practicality of sun-reactive skin types I through VI. Arch Dermatol. 1988 Jun;124(6):869–71.

66.

Tired doctors 'fall asleep driving' [Internet]. BBC News. [cited 2020 Feb 13]. Available from: https://www.bbc.com/news/av/uk-england-berkshire-38716140/doctors-fall-asleep-driving-after-punishing-night-shifts-the-bbc-learns

67.

Ofoma UR, Basnet S, Berger A, Kirchner HL, Girotra S, Investigators for the AHAGW the G-R, et al. Trends in Survival After In-Hospital Cardiac Arrest During Nights and Weekends. J Am Coll Cardiol. 2018 Jan 22;71(4):402–11.

68.

Ahmad AS, Ormiston-Smith N, Sasieni PD. Trends in the lifetime risk of developing cancer in Great Britain: comparison of risk for those born from 1930 to 1960. British Journal of Cancer. 2015 Mar;112(5):943–7.

69.

Moberly T. UK has fewer doctors per person than most other OECD countries. BMJ [Internet]. 2017 Jun 20 [cited 2020 Feb 13];357. Available from: https://www.bmj.com/content/357/bmj.j2940

70.

Alang N, Kelly CR. Weight Gain After Fecal Microbiota Transplantation. Open Forum Infect Dis [Internet]. 2015 Feb 1 [cited 2020 Feb 12];2(1). Available from: https://www.ncbi.nlm.nih.gov/pmc/articles/PMC4438885/

71.

Natarajan V. What Einstein meant when he said 'God does not play dice ...' arXiv:13011656 [physics] [Internet]. 2013 Jan 5 [cited 2020 Feb 13]; Available from: http://arxiv.org/abs/1301.1656

Printed in Great Britain
by Amazon

16676491R00078